MAXWELL HOUSE®

coffee drinks
& desserts
cookbook

From Lattes and Muffins to Decadent Cakes and Midnight Treats

MAXWELL HOUSE®
coffee drinks
& desserts
cookbook

From Lattes and Muffins to Decadent Cakes and Midnight Treats

Original recipes by the Maxwell House Creative Kitchens

Edited by Barbara Albright

Photographs by John Uher

Clarkson Potter / Publishers

New York

credits

THE MAXWELL HOUSE CREATIVE KITCHENS—
Recipe Development and Testing
Division Manager: Theresa Ann Kreinen
Consumer Food Manager: Mary Beth Harrington
Kitchen Technician: Mary J. Bailey
Kitchen Technician: LaVon L. James

THE MAXWELL HOUSE TEAM
President, Maxwell House Coffee Company: Ann Fudge
Vice President Marketing: Erv Frederick
Senior Brand Manager: Angela Crawford
Associate Brand Manager: Jerry Densk
Associate Brand Manager: Yvonne Gerald
Category Promotion Manager: Kathy Heller

CLARKSON POTTER / PUBLISHERS
The Crown Publishing Group
President and Publisher: Chip Gibson
Vice President-Editorial Director: Lauren Shakely
Senior Production Manager: Jane Searle
Senior Editor: Katie Workman
Editorial Assistant: Julia Coblentz
Managing Editor: Amy Boorstein

LIFETIME MEDIA, INC.
President: Jacqueline Varoli
Editor: Ruth Greenstein
Copy Editor: Jean Atcheson

Photographer: John Uher
Assistant Photographer: Michelle Edwards
Assistant Photographer: Robert Piazza
Food Stylist: Liz Duffy
Assistant Food Stylist: Leeanne Loftfield
Assistant Food Stylist: Joyce Sangirardi
Prop Stylist: Ina Slote

Tableware generously provided by:
Annieglass ✦ Crate & Barrel ✦ Dansk ✦ Lenox Crystal ✦
Vietri, Inc. ✦ Villeroy & Boch Tableware, Inc. ✦ Wedgwood USA

Front cover photograph: Chocolate Toffee Bars
Title page photograph: Hot Coffee Float

Prepared and produced by LifeTime Media, Inc., 352 Seventh Avenue, New York, New York 10001, (212) 684-1900, www.lifetimemedia.com

Published by Clarkson Potter/Publishers, 201 East 50th Street, New York, New York 10022. Member of the Crown Publishing Group.
Random House, Inc. New York, Toronto, London, Sydney, Auckland
www.randomhouse.com
CLARKSON POTTER, POTTER, and colophon are registered trademarks of Random House, Inc.

MAXWELL HOUSE®, "Good to the last drop!®", and the cup and drop logo are registered trademarks of Kraft Foods, Inc.

Printed in Japan

Library of Congress Cataloging-in-Publication Data is available upon request.

ISBN 0-609-60542-9

10 9 8 7 6 5 4 3 2 1

First Edition

For coffee, chocolate, and
dessert lovers everywhere

table of contents

foreword

By Ann Fudge, President,
Maxwell House Coffee Company

I love coffee and I love desserts! Both give me a chance to spend time with family and friends, sharing conversation or simply enjoying the pleasure of their company.

Wonderfully tantalizing desserts are an American favorite and are often enjoyed with coffee. At Maxwell House, we have recognized that in addition to drinking coffee with desserts, coffee is a natural partner with many dessert ingredients including chocolate, whipped cream, pudding and nuts. This insight led to the creation of the first ever Maxwell House cookbook dedicated *exclusively* to drinks and desserts made with coffee. I am delighted to share these wonderful recipes with you.

Maxwell House Coffee Drinks and Desserts brings an unexpected twist to enjoying coffee. Our imaginative food professionals in the Maxwell House Creative Kitchens have spent many hours testing and re-testing recipes to come up with over 160 original dessert creations. These exciting recipes will allow you to experience coffee as never before.

The theme of our book is "Around the Clock." Categorized by time of day, the recipes are designed to deliciously demonstrate that coffee and coffee-flavored desserts are great at any time. Whether for *Breakfast or Brunch*, a *Coffee Break*, *Lunch*, *Afternoon Coffee Time*, *Dinner*, *After the Show* or a *Midnight Snack*, you can enjoy coffee day or night. The desserts in this book are sophisticated yet easy to make. Each recipe offers a unique taste experience. We have included exciting recipes that you can put together in ten minutes or less to serve to your family and friends — or just as a treat to yourself. There are also some show-stoppers — unexpected combinations that you can put together to delight even the most discerning dessert lover!

I am very pleased that you have decided to try *Maxwell House Coffee Drinks and Desserts* and hope these recipes become a part of your favorite dessert collection. I'm sure you will find that Maxwell House coffee is good at any time of the day and is always…. Good to the last drop!®

all about
coffee

At the time of its discovery, coffee was not only savored by
many people around the world but was also imbued with
mystical powers. In the eighteenth century, coffee houses became
home to literary and political discussions, and
sipping coffee inspired artists, physicians,
students, and religious leaders to debate into the wee
hours of the morning.
Today millions of people enjoy coffee in many different
forms. The following pages provide a glimpse of the
history of coffee and the story of Maxwell House,
along with helpful hints on brewing perfect coffee
and valuable tips for making
delectable desserts.

the history of coffee

How Coffee Came to Be

Sometime around 1000 A.D., in the earliest days of coffee's history, Arab traders brought coffee beans to Arabia. It would be at least four centuries before the bushes were cultivated there extensively. Coffee plantations came into being after a visionary in Persia, now Iran, hit on the idea of roasting the beans, grinding them, and brewing them with boiling water into the beverage we know as coffee.

By the sixteenth century, the knowledge of coffee and its allure had spread throughout the Arab world. Coffee houses appeared in Mecca itself and coffee and the rituals surrounding its drinking became central to daily life.

In the seventeenth century, coffee rapidly became a popular and fashionable European drink. In London and Paris, the new coffeehouses almost immediately blossomed into thriving businesses and meeting places for the political, social, and literary intelligentsia of the day. Vienna, which would become famous for its coffee houses, had caught up with the new fashion by 1683. The Dutch introduced coffee plantations in their colonies in the East and West Indies, and it was they who were responsible for bringing coffee to the New World.

The custom of drinking coffee reached the American colonies in the late 1600s, and coffee houses sprang up and flourished in New York, Boston, and Philadelphia. A full century had to pass, however, before drinking coffee became so widely popular that it eventually displaced beer as the first drink of the day.

In pioneer days, the grinding and roasting of coffee was an important morning routine even on the trail, and native coffee drinking traditions and rituals accompanied North America's push westward. By this time, coffee was being grown on plantations in Central and South America, where the tropical temperatures and mountainous topography were (and are) ideal for its cultivation.

Today, more than a third of the world's population considers coffee an enjoyable part of everyday life.

The Scoop on Coffee

Coffee grows best in the so-called coffee belt — an area that encircles the globe and is roughly banded by the tropics of Cancer and Capricorn, from about 25 latitude degrees north to 30 degrees south of the equator. The coffee-growing regions are Central and South America, East Africa, and Indonesia.

Central and South American coffees are light- to medium-bodied with clean, lively flavors. African coffees have unique floral and wine notes, and are typically medium- to full-bodied. Indonesian coffees are full-bodied with exotic elements. Coffee contains as many as 800 elements, making its flavor as fascinatingly complex as the finest wines.

The coffee tree is a bushy evergreen that grows to a height of 10 to 20 feet. The pyramid-shaped trees have slender, shiny green leaves that are paired along the branches. Newly planted trees do not begin to bear fruit for five or six years, but once the trees are mature, they may remain productive for more than 30 years.

Coffee trees produce a spectacular flowering of fragrant white blossoms that fill the air with an intense scent like jasmine. These flowers produce oval "cherries" that turn dark red or yellow, depending on the variety. Each cherry contains two pale green seeds within a tough parchment-like covering.

In most countries, coffee is harvested when almost all of the cherries are ripe. A single branch can bear flowers, green cherries, and ripened cherries simultaneously. Since the cherries ripen at varying times, the majority of picking is still done by hand, though mechanical harvesters are increasingly being used. Higher quality beans are picked only when the beans are ripe and are always hand picked.

After harvesting, the cherries are cleaned and the covering is removed from the beans, which are then dried, sorted, graded, and packed in bags. The beans are not roasted until they reach their final destination.

The bulk of the coffee beans that come into the United States come from just two: *Coffea Arabica*, and *Coffea Robusta*. The arabica, grown at high altitudes, is the best, low-yielding, and most expensive bean for fine coffees. The robusta, from a heartier tree, is less costly, high-yielding, and destined for blends, instants, and decafs.

In the roasting process, the beans are heated in cylindrical ovens, cooled immediately to minimize the loss of aromatic substances. Roasting caramelizes the beans' natural sugars, which changes their color from greenish-gray to brown, and they lose 15 to 20 percent of their original weight. The process also causes volatile essential oils and fatty acids to rise to the surface, giving the beans their distinctive flavor and aroma. The longer they are roasted, the more bitter—but less acidic—they become. It takes about 2,000 beans to make five pounds of coffee.

Instant coffee is made from ground roasted beans that have been percolated to produce a coffee extract. The liquid is then deyhdrated to form a powder that can be reconstituted by adding boiling water.

Learning the Lingo

There are a host of variations on that old black magic, which basically comes in three forms: black, white, and extra strong. Each nation has its own style of brewing the coffee, by stirring, dripping, filtering, or forcing boiling water through the grounds, and of serving it with milk or cream, hot or cold, steamed, frothed, or whipped, and adding flavorings. Many new American favorites are originally Italian and based on espresso.

Caffé Americano—espresso diluted with boiling water to more or less the strength of regular American coffee. (Only a portion of the water is forced through the grounds in order to extract the full coffee flavor while leaving behind the bitter oils.)

Caffé Breve—espresso made with steamed half-and-half.

Caffé con Panna—espresso topped with whipped cream.

Caffé Correcto—espresso corrected with a small quantity of grappa, Cognac, Sambuca, or other spirit.

Caffé Freddo—chilled espresso served in a chilled glass.

Caffé Latte—espresso made with 75 percent steamed, frothy milk. *Café au Lait*, the French version, is strong filtered coffee with 25 percent hot milk added, served in an extra-large cup. *Café con Leche* is Spanish-style espresso made with steamed milk.

Caffé Mocha—espresso with cocoa or chocolate syrup and steamed milk, topped with whipped cream.

Caffé Ristretto—a concentrated espresso made with less than the customary quantity of water.

Cappuccino—espresso topped with a "cap" of foamed milk. The name comes from the Capuchin Friars, an order founded by St. Francis of Assisi, who wore brown robes with hoods known familiarly as *cappuccinos*.

Cappuccino Chiaro—a light cappuccino made with a small quantity of ground coffee beans.

Cappuccino Scuro—a dark, very strong cappuccino made with a larger than traditional quantity of ground coffee beans.

Crema—the thin layer of dense, creamy-brown froth or foam on the top of well-made espresso. Italian connoisseurs judge their espresso by the quantity and quality of the crema.

Demitasse—the French word for half a cup. It refers to the small cups in which espresso in Italy and after-dinner coffee in France are traditionally served.

Doppio—a double espresso; a 3-ounce serving.

Espresso—strong, concentrated coffee made by forcing boiling water, under pressure, through finely ground, medium-to-dark roasted beans. Traditionally, a serving is 1½ ounces.

Espresso Macchiato—espresso with just a touch of foamed milk.

Espresso Romano—espresso with a strip of lemon peel.

Flavored Latte—espresso-based caffé latte flavored with a sweet syrup.

Half-Caf—espresso, latte, or cappuccino made with half caffeinated and half decaffeinated coffee.

Latte Macchiato—steamed, frothy milk through which is poured a small quantity of espresso.

Red Eye—a cup of regular coffee with a demitasse of espresso added.

Skinny—cappuccino or latte topped with steamed skim milk.

SPEAKING THE LINGO

The word for coffee is remarkably similar in several languages.

Café—French, Spanish, and Portuguese
Caffé—Italian
Kafes—Greek
Kaffe—Swedish and Danish
Kaffee—German
Kahveh *or* **Kavé**—Turkish
Kofe *or* **Kophe**—Russian
Koffie—Dutch
Koohii—Japanese

the Maxwell House story

The Maxwell House Coffee Company began during the Reconstruction years that followed the Civil War. In those days, when a boy celebrated coming of age on his 21st birthday, his father presented him with a silver dollar — called a freedom dollar — as a symbol of his independence. The now adult son was free to venture forth on his own. In 1873, Joel Cheek, carrying his freedom dollar, left the family farm in Kentucky and rafted down the Cumberland River to Nashville, Tennessee. There he found a job as a traveling salesman for a wholesale grocery firm. Riding on horseback, he carried product samples, including coffee, in his saddlebags.

Cheek was an able salesman with high standards and within a decade he was made a partner in the firm. But he was determined to sell only products that he thought were top-notch and he was not happy with the quality of the firm's coffee. During his time off from work, he began to experiment to concoct what he would consider a perfect blend of coffee. For years he roasted samples, blending varieties repeatedly until he had handcrafted a brew that satisfied him. Then he convinced Nashville's newest and most exclusive hotel, the Maxwell House, to give his newly designed blend a taste test. Soon the hotel's customers were praising its rich flavor and deeming it the ideal coffee to go with the Maxwell House's highly acclaimed cuisine. In 1892, the Maxwell House managers agreed to lend its name to the special blend of coffee served there.

From that point on, Cheek's business expanded rapidly. Spurred on by the increasing popularity of his Maxwell House coffee, Cheek and a new partner started their own wholesale grocery firm specializing in coffee, and soon joined forces with John Neal, one of his former salesmen, to seek a wider market for the company and its now world-famous brew. In 1901, Cheek and Neal formed the Nashville Coffee and Manufacturing Company and started manufacturing Maxwell House coffee in a specially constructed plant on North Market Street in Nashville. In 1905 they changed the firm's name to the Cheek-Neal Coffee Company and opened a second plant in Houston, Texas.

President Theodore Roosevelt tasted Maxwell House coffee while on a visit to Nashville in 1907 and legend has it that he proclaimed his cup of coffee was "good to the last drop." This casually made comment soon became trademarked as the brand's most recognizable advertising slogan.

Over the next 20 years, the Cheek-Neal Coffee Company built Maxwell House into a national brand, adding manufacturing plants in Florida, Virginia, and New York, as well as Los Angeles and Chicago. Then, in 1928, it became part of the General Foods Corporation (now Kraft Foods, Inc.) and embarked on yet another stage of growth.

Throughout the 1930s, experiments were made to invent a completely new type of coffee product — one that would not have to be brewed, but could be made just by adding hot water. The going was slow as the Maxwell House researchers perfected this breakthrough technology. Finally, in 1942, the company achieved its goal of "instant" coffee — and immediately began shipping the total supply overseas to supply the American troops fighting in World War II. After the war, Maxwell House Instant Coffee became available to the general public for the first time.

Throughout the following decades, Maxwell House has continued to develop coffee products for the way Americans *really* live. Many improvements have been made in the processing and packing methods and even in the blend to keep pace with the nation's ever-changing taste for good coffee. When electric percolators became widely used, Maxwell House accommodated coffee drinkers with its 1966 product Electra-Perk, the first coffee designed specifically for this use. More recently, coffee connoisseurs have appreciated the rich taste of premium products such as Maxwell House Italian Espresso Roast, Colombian Supreme, Rich French Roast, Maxwell House Lite, Master Blend, Maxwell House 1892, Maxwell House Slow Roast, and, of course, regular Maxwell House Coffee. The

beans for these fine coffees are blended, roasted, and ground at three plant locations: Jacksonville, Florida; Houston, Texas; and San Leandro, California.

In addition, the company has continued to keep track of the way consumers drink coffee today and the latest expansions of the brand include a variety of instant coffees and decaffeinated coffees, filter packs, and a line of flavored cappuccino mixes. With an eye toward the future, Maxwell House will continue to make coffee, just the way Americans want it.

brewing and serving
tips and tricks

Brewing the Perfect Pot of Coffee

Making a great pot of coffee becomes easier when you start with a great coffee. To ensure that you get the best results and make a pot that's always…"Good to the last drop!®," here are the easy steps to follow:

✦ Start with fresh, cold water and bring it to boil. Immediately pour the boiling water over the ground coffee

✦ Be precise when you measure both the coffee and the water. A proper balance helps make a perfect cup of coffee. Use a standard coffee measure (2 level measuring tablespoons) and allow 6 fluid ounces of water per measure of coffee.

✦ Use the correct grind for your coffee maker and follow the manufacturer's instructions.

✦ Serve the coffee as soon as possible to preserve its aroma and flavor. Freshly brewed means fresh taste. Coffee can be kept warm only for about 20 minutes before the flavor starts to deteriorate. If you must keep it hot, use a vacuum carafe or flask.

✦ Keep your coffee fresh. Buy only a week's supply at a time. Store ground coffee in a tightly covered container in your refrigerator. To keep it longer than two weeks, store the container in the freezer.

✦ Use the right equipment. Make sure that your coffee maker is clean to ensure that it brews a cup of coffee that is always…"Good to the last drop!®."

✦ Never serve reheated coffee.

Serving Coffee with Style

A cup of coffee becomes extra-special when you have the right accompaniments to go along with it. A cup of coffee is usually the finale to a meal you have prepared with care, and when it is served with style and pizzazz, coffee makes a lasting impression.

Here are some ideas to help you present coffee: Collect an assortment of different sizes and styles of coffee cups. Don't be afraid to mix and match the cups, but keep each cup with its appropriate saucer. You might want to select a theme such as all white cups, blue and white cups, or cups with a floral motif.

Keep a coffee tray ready to go. The tray could include cups and saucers, spoons, a sugar bowl, a creamer, and napkins. Some extra items to consider adding: raw sugar, brown sugar, sugar cubes with tongs, artificial sweetener, cinnamon sticks, crystallized ginger, and a shaker filled with ground cinnamon for sprinkling on top of the coffee. (Turn to page 20 for some great ideas for chocolate decorations.) You might like to present a selection of liqueurs or flavored syrups. Just before serving, pour milk or half-and-half into the creamer, and offer whipped cream and lemon peel strips for guests to add to their coffee if they wish.

Today you can choose from a full repertoire of coffees for every occasion—when you drink coffee or use it in a recipe. There will be slight variations in the taste of the recipes in this cookbook, depending on the variety of coffee you use. The Maxwell House Creative Kitchens professionals suggest the following varieties: Regular Maxwell House, Master Blend, and Maxwell House Slow Roast for a balanced blend and smooth taste; Maxwell House 1892 for a fuller bodied aromatic flavor; Rich French Roast, Colombian Supreme, and Italian Espresso Roast for a stronger, richer taste; and Maxwell House Lite for half the caffeine.

You can also choose from a variety of instant coffees and cappuccino mixes, and of course, you can use any decaffeinated variety as a substitute.

In this recipe book, liquid coffee is used as an ingredient in the following strengths: "Regular," "Strong," and "Double-Strength." Below are instructions for making the various strengths using both ground and instant coffee.

In some recipes, instant coffee is added in the dry form. This is described as instant coffee. Do not add regular coffee grounds to these recipes.

Using Coffee in this Book

GROUND COFFEE USAGE INSTRUCTIONS:

Strength	Amount of Ground Coffee	Amount of Water
REGULAR	1 tablespoon	3/4 cup (6 fl. oz.)
	1/4 cup	3 cups
	1/2 cup	7 1/2 cups
STRONG	1 1/2 tablespoons	3/4 cup (6 fl. oz.)
	1/3 cup	3 cups
	3/4 cup	7 1/2 cups
DOUBLE-STRENGTH	2 tablespoons	3/4 cup (6 fl. oz.)
	1/2 cup	3 cups
	1 cup	7 1/2 cups

INSTANT COFFEE USAGE INSTRUCTIONS:

Strength	Amount of Instant Coffee	Amount of Water
REGULAR	1 teaspoon	3/4 cup (6 fl. oz.)
	2 teaspoons	1 1/2 cups
STRONG	1 1/2 teaspoons	3/4 cup (6 fl. oz.)
	3 teaspoons	1 1/2 cups
DOUBLE-STRENGTH	2 teaspoons	3/4 cup (6 fl. oz.)
	4 teaspoons	1 1/2 cups

at home in the kitchen

How to Guarantee Delicious Desserts

As everyone has heard but tends to forget, it is well worth the time to read the recipe carefully before getting started. Then assemble all the ingredients and the equipment and prepare the pan if necessary.

Measure all of the ingredients carefully. Use a glass "liquid" measuring cup to measure liquids and a set of "dry" measuring cups to measure dry ingredients. Always use measuring spoons, not flatware. Level off measuring spoons and dry measuring cups with the flat edge of a metal spatula or a knife. Read measurements for liquid ingredients at eye level. (Refer to individual ingredients for specific instructions.)

For best results, position your oven rack so that baked goods are baked in the center of the oven. If you are baking more than one pan, space the racks evenly. Preheat the oven to the specified temperature and use an oven thermometer to check the temperature of your oven. Each recipe gives an approximate time amount as well as a visual test for doneness. If a range of times is given, check for doneness at the earliest time given.

Ingredients

Coffee

All of the recipes in this book have been carefully created and tested using Maxwell House Coffee products. (See page 17 for descriptions of the various coffee products.)

Flour

The recipes in this book use all-purpose flour. To measure flour, lightly spoon the flour into the appropriate dry measuring cup(s). Try not to be heavy-handed. Level it off with the straight edge of a metal spatula or a knife. Do not tap the cup or dip it into the flour or you will end up with more flour than is needed.

Sugar

These recipes use granulated sugar, powdered sugar, and brown sugar. In addition to adding sweetness, sugar contributes to the texture of desserts. Measure sugar by filling the appropriate dry measuring cup(s). Level it off with the straight edge of a metal spatula or a knife. Measure powdered sugar in the same way that you measure flour. Light and dark brown sugar are interchangeable in recipes. Dark brown sugar will produce a darker dessert than light brown sugar (if there isn't some other darker ingredient such as chocolate or coffee). To measure brown sugar, press it firmly into the appropriate size dry measuring cup(s) until it is level with the top edge. It should hold the form of the cup when it is turned out.

Store brown sugar in an airtight container in a cool place. If your brown sugar becomes hard, softening directions are usually given on the package. One method is to place the brown sugar in a tightly covered plastic container. Cover the surface with a piece of plastic wrap and then top it with a folded moist paper towel. Seal the container for 8 to 12 hours before removing the towel.

Baking Powder and Baking Soda

These two items are not interchangeable. Use which ever is called for in the recipe. Use double-acting baking powder, which is the type most readily available. Double-acting baking powder enables leavening to occur both at room temperature and during baking.

When acid ingredients, such as buttermilk, sour cream, yogurt, or cranberries, are used in baking, it is usually necessary to add baking soda. Make sure your baking powder and baking soda are fresh. They can lose their leavening ability if they are stored past the expiration date or if moisture gets into the container.

Salt

These recipes use very little salt and when divided among the servings, the amount of salt is minimal. Don't leave it out. Just a little bit greatly enhances the flavor of most baked goods.

Eggs

Select large, uncracked eggs. Let the eggs reach room temperature before using so that they incorporate better with the other ingredients. To quickly bring eggs to room temperature, submerge them in a bowl of very warm water. Do not let eggs stand at room temperature for more than 2 hours. Because salmonella could be present in raw eggs, it is not advisable to taste any mixture containing uncooked eggs. Always cook eggs to 160°F to reduce any risk of salmonella.

Butter

Butter and margarine can be used interchangeably in these recipes. Do not substitute tub margarines, spreads, or vegetable oils.

Vanilla

Always use pure vanilla extract to ensure the best taste. Vanilla adds a full, rich flavor to coffee and to coffee recipes.

Spices

Store spices in airtight containers away from light and heat. Older spices lose their potency, so it is a good idea to date your containers at the time of purchase.

Corn Syrup

Use the type of corn syrup specified if one is given. In most cases, either light or dark can be used.

Chocolate and Cocoa Powder

All of the recipes in this book were developed using Baker's Chocolate squares. Use the type of chocolate specified: Unsweetened Chocolate, German's Sweet Chocolate, Semi-Sweet Chocolate, Bittersweet Chocolate, or White Chocolate.

The cocoa powder used in this book is the unsweetened variety.

Fruits

Use the fruits called for in each recipe. For instance, do not substitute chopped fresh fruit for dried fruit and vice versa. In many cases, you can substitute an equal amount of one variety of dried fruit for another variety of dried fruit.

Peanut Butter

Use commercially prepared peanut butter (not reduced-fat). The health food store type may change the texture of the recipe.

Nuts

Taste nuts before you use them in recipes as they can become rancid and spoil your recipes. Store nuts in airtight containers in the refrigerator or freezer.

Tips and Techniques

It is often the little things that make the difference between an ordinary dessert and an extraordinary dessert. Here are some easy suggestions that will elevate you to "dessert maker" extraordinaire.

Sweetened Whipped Cream

Sweetened whipped cream is a delightful topping for almost every dessert and goes well with most coffee drinks. Beat 1 cup of cold heavy (whipping) cream in a chilled bowl using chilled beaters until frothy. Gradually beat in 2 tablespoons of granulated sugar or ¼ cup of powdered sugar and ½ teaspoon of vanilla extract and continue beating just until the mixture forms smooth glossy peaks. It is best served immediately, but you can also store it in the refrigerator and beat it a few times with a wire whisk just before serving to restore its texture. You can also omit the sugar and vanilla, if desired, or double the recipe.

For an extra-special treat, place the whipped cream in a pastry bag fitted with a decorative tip and pipe decorative borders and dollops on desserts and beverages. You can also pipe individual dollops onto a wax-paper-lined baking sheet and freeze them until firm. Wrap the dollops individually and store them in a tightly covered container in the freezer. Use the dollops to top beverages or desserts.

Grating Chocolate

Grate only 1 square (1 ounce) of semi-sweet or bittersweet chocolate or half a package of German's sweet chocolate at a time over the large holes of a hand grater. Sprinkle the grated chocolate over cakes, pies, desserts, and beverages. Grated chocolate looks especially inviting when sprinkled on whipped cream or whipped topping.

Shaving Chocolate

Pull a vegetable peeler across the surface of 1 square (1 ounce) of semi-sweet or bittersweet chocolate or a 3-square strip of German's sweet chocolate. Sprinkle the shaved chocolate on cakes, pies, desserts, and beverages.

Chocolate Curls

Melt 4 squares (4 ounces) of semi-sweet or bittersweet chocolate or 1 package (4 ounces) of German's sweet chocolate. Using a spatula, spread the chocolate in a very thin layer on a baking sheet. Refrigerate for about 10 minutes or until firm, but still pliable.

To make curls, slip the tip of a straight-sided metal spatula under the chocolate. Push the spatula firmly along the baking sheet until the chocolate curls as it is pushed. (If the chocolate is too firm to curl, let it stand for a few minutes at room temperature; refrigerate again if it becomes too soft.) Carefully pick up each chocolate curl by inserting a wooden pick in the center. Lift onto a wax-paper-lined baking sheet. Refrigerate about 15 minutes or until firm. Lift with a wooden pick to prevent breakage or melting. Freeze or refrigerate in a tightly covered container until ready to use. Use to decorate cakes, pies, desserts, and beverages.

Chocolate Drizzle

Place 1 square (1 ounce) semi-sweet or bittersweet chocolate in a freezer-weight zipper-style plastic sandwich bag. Close the bag tightly. Microwave on High for about 1 minute or until the chocolate is melted. Fold down the top of the bag tightly and snip a tiny piece off one corner (about ⅛ inch).

Holding the top of the bag tightly, drizzle the chocolate through the opening over brownies, cookies, cakes, pies, or desserts.

coffee around
the clock

Before sunrise, the rich aroma of freshly made coffee heralds the start of a new
day. Lingering after sunset with an evening cup of coffee and a sweet treat
can also make for a relaxing finish to the day. As coffee lovers know, coffee
and coffee-flavored desserts are perfect "Around the Clock."
Each of the following seven chapters is filled to the brim with decadent
and delicious desserts and coffees well-suited to a particular
time of the day.
The recipes have been graded according to their level of complexity.
One coffee cup ⟋ represents the simplest recipes—they are very easy
and can be made in less than 10 minutes. For anyone who enjoys cooking
and baking, two-cup recipes ⟋ ⟋ are still simple to make. Three-cup
recipes ⟋ ⟋ ⟋ are slightly more challenging—they may require a few more
ingredients or preparation steps, and may take a little longer to make.
Four cups ⟋ ⟋ ⟋ ⟋ mark recipes that require some culinary know-how,
a little more time, and possibly some advance preparation.
Of course, almost all of the recipes can be enjoyed at any time throughout
the day, but we hope our suggestions will inspire you to think coffee
"Around the Clock.

breakfast &
brunch

Time—the availability or lack of it—spells the difference between breakfast and brunch. For a fast early-morning energizer try the *shake awake smoothie* (page 26).

Or, if you organize the ingredients the night before, you can even quickly bake some *coffee bran muffins* (page 24) while you are in the shower.

If you do have some extra time, invite some friends over to enjoy a *coffee angel pie* (page 39).

And it's hard to beat a mug of *spiced orange coffee* (page 33) to keep you company along with the Sunday newspaper.

coffee bran muffins
swedish almond toasts
shake awake smoothie
cocoa java
maple cinnamon coffee
café au lait
coffee crumb cake
cranberry breakfast biscotti
coffee date nut bread
coffee maple butter
spiced orange coffee
mocha punch
sour cream streusel coffee cake
carrot cake
coffee cream cheese frosting
coffee angel food cake
coffee angel pie
chocolate nut loaves
spiced apple coffee cake
shortcakes with espresso cream
easy coffee pound cake
hawaiian dessert sauce
mocha sauce

coffee bran muffins

Bring a batch of these to any morning get-together along with
Coffee Cream Cheese (page 56).

Prep: 15 minutes • Bake: 25 minutes

1 ⅓ cups all-purpose flour
1 teaspoon baking soda
1 ½ cups 100% bran cereal
1 cup buttermilk
½ cup granulated sugar
¼ cup (½ stick) butter *or* margarine, softened
½ cup room temperature brewed strong coffee
¼ cup dark corn syrup
1 large egg
¾ cup raisins

✦ **HEAT** the oven to 375°F. Lightly butter 12 muffin pan cups (or line them with paper cups).

✦ **MIX** the flour and baking soda in a small bowl. Stir the cereal and buttermilk in another bowl; let stand for 5 minutes.

✦ **BEAT** the sugar and butter in a large bowl with an electric mixer set on medium speed until light and fluffy. Add the coffee, corn syrup, and egg and beat until smooth. Stir in the flour and cereal mixtures just until moistened. (The batter will be lumpy.) Stir in the raisins. Spoon the batter into the prepared muffin cups, filling each cup two-thirds full.

✦ **BAKE** for 25 minutes or until a toothpick inserted in the center of one muffin comes out clean. Remove the pan to a wire rack and cool for 5 minutes. Remove the muffins from the pan and cool completely on the wire rack. Serve warm.

Makes 1 dozen muffins

swedish almond toasts

Serve these crisp cookies to accompany a freshly made, specially appreciated morning cup of coffee.

Prep: 20 minutes • Bake: 50 to 60 minutes

2 large eggs
1 tablespoon instant coffee
1/4 teaspoon vanilla extract
2 cups all-purpose flour
1/2 teaspoon baking powder
1/4 teaspoon salt
1/2 cup (1 stick) butter *or* margarine, softened
1 cup granulated sugar
1/2 cup finely chopped blanched almonds

✦ **HEAT** the oven to 350°F. Lightly butter and flour a large baking sheet.

✦ **STIR** the eggs, instant coffee, and vanilla in a small bowl until well blended; set aside. Mix the flour, baking powder, and salt in a medium bowl; set aside.

✦ **BEAT** the butter and sugar in a large bowl with an electric mixer set on medium speed until light and fluffy. Beat in the egg mixture. Gradually add the flour mixture, beating well after each addition. Stir in the almonds.

✦ **DIVIDE** the dough into 2 equal portions. On a lightly floured surface, shape the dough into 2 logs, each 8 inches long, 2 inches wide, and 1 inch thick. Place the logs 2 inches apart on the prepared baking sheet.

✦ **BAKE** for 30 to 40 minutes or until lightly browned. Set the baking sheet on a wire rack to cool for 10 minutes. Remove the logs from the baking sheet and place on a cutting board. Using a serrated knife, cut each log diagonally into 3/4-inch-thick slices. Place the slices upright and 1/2-inch apart on the baking sheet. Bake for 20 minutes or until slightly dry. Remove the toasts from the baking sheet. Cool completely on the wire rack. Store in a tightly covered container.

Makes about 3 1/2 dozen toasts

shake awake
smoothie

Here's a smoothie that will get you up and going in the morning.

Prep: 5 minutes

1 cup cold brewed double-strength coffee

1 banana

1 container (8 ounces) vanilla lowfat yogurt

2 teaspoons granulated sugar

¼ cup ice cubes

◆ **PLACE** all of the ingredients in a blender container; cover. Blend on high speed until smooth. Pour into tall glasses. Serve immediately.

Makes 2 servings

cocoa java

Hot cocoa and coffee combine to make a beverage that tastes equally good hot or cold.

Prep: 5 minutes

4 envelopes (1 ounce each) instant hot cocoa mix (¾ cup)

3 cups hot freshly brewed coffee

◆ **POUR** the cocoa mix into a large heatproof pitcher. Add the coffee and stir until dissolved. Pour into large cups or mugs.

Makes 4 servings

COFFEE HOUSE INSPIRATIONS

For a Single Serving, pour 1 envelope of hot cocoa mix into a large cup or mug. Add the hot freshly brewed coffee and stir until dissolved.

For a Cool Variation, prepare the beverage as directed and refrigerate. Serve over ice.

shake awake smoothie

maple cinnamon coffee

Maple-flavored syrup and cinnamon combine to make a cozy and comforting beverage.

Prep: 5 minutes

6 tablespoons ground coffee
½ teaspoon ground cinnamon
½ cup maple-flavored syrup
4½ cups cold water
Whipped cream (optional)

✦ **PLACE** the coffee and cinnamon in the filter in the brew basket of a coffee maker. Pour the syrup into the empty pot of the coffee maker.

✦ **PREPARE** the coffee with the cold water. When the brewing is complete, stir until well mixed. Pour into large cups or mugs. Top with whipped cream, if desired.

Makes 6 servings

café au lait

This hot coffee beverage will transport you to a corner café in Paris.

Prep: 5 minutes

1 cup ground coffee
4 cups cold water
4 cups milk, heated

✦ **PREPARE** the coffee with the cold water in a coffee maker. To serve, pour equal amounts of brewed coffee and hot milk into mugs or cups. Sweeten to taste, if desired.

Makes about 8 servings

coffee crumb cake

A cake mix makes this recipe really easy to prepare. It is generously topped with a brown sugar and cinnamon streusel mixture.

Prep: 15 minutes • Bake: 40 minutes

1 package (2-layer size) yellow cake mix

Cold brewed strong coffee

2 cups all-purpose flour

½ cup firmly packed brown sugar

½ cup granulated sugar

1 tablespoon instant coffee

¼ teaspoon ground cinnamon

1 cup (2 sticks) butter *or* margarine, softened, cut into chunks

✦ **HEAT** the oven to 350°F.

✦ **PREPARE** the cake mix as directed on the package for a 15x10x1-inch baking pan, substituting the brewed coffee for the water. Bake for 20 minutes.

✦ **MEANWHILE**, mix the flour, sugars, instant coffee, and cinnamon in a large bowl. Using a pastry blender or 2 knives, cut in the butter until the mixture resembles coarse crumbs. Sprinkle the crumb mixture evenly over the cake.

✦ **BAKE** for 20 minutes longer or until a toothpick inserted in the center comes out clean. Cool on a wire rack. Cut into squares to serve.

Makes 24 servings

A DROP OF HISTORY

1852   Joel Owsley Cheek, the father of Maxwell House coffee, is born in Burkesville, Kentucky, on December 8.

1859   Plans are instituted to build a new hotel called the Maxwell House in Nashville, Tennessee, but progress is soon interrupted by the outbreak of the Civil War.

cranberry
breakfast biscotti

Tangy cranberries punctuate these crisp, coffee-flavored biscotti.
Tuck a couple of them in your pocket for a breakfast-on-the-run.

Prep: 20 minutes • Bake: 35 minutes

2 large eggs
2 tablespoons instant coffee
1 teaspoon vanilla extract
2 cups all-purpose flour
1½ teaspoons baking powder
¼ teaspoon salt
½ cup (1 stick) butter *or* margarine, softened
¾ cup granulated sugar
1½ cups dried cranberries
Melted white *or* semi-sweet chocolate for
    drizzling on top of the biscotti (optional)

✦ **HEAT** the oven to 325°F. Lightly butter and flour
a large baking sheet.

✦ **STIR** the eggs, instant coffee, and vanilla in a small
bowl until well blended; set aside. Mix the flour,
baking powder, and salt in a medium bowl; set aside.

✦ **BEAT** the butter and sugar in a large bowl with an
electric mixer set on medium speed until light and
fluffy. Beat in the egg mixture. Gradually add the
flour mixture, beating well after each addition. Stir
in the cranberries.

cranberry breakfast biscotti and
maple cinnamon coffee (page 28)

✦ **DIVIDE** the dough into 2 equal portions. On a
lightly floured surface, shape the dough into 2 logs,
each 14 inches long, 1½ inches wide, and 1 inch
thick. Place the logs 2 inches apart on the prepared
baking sheet.

✦ **BAKE** for 25 minutes or until lightly browned.
Set the baking sheet on a wire rack to cool for
10 minutes. Remove the logs from the baking sheet
and place on a cutting board. Using a serrated knife,
cut each log diagonally into ¾-inch-thick slices.
Place the slices upright and ½ inch apart on the
baking sheet. Bake for 10 minutes or until slightly
dry. Remove the biscotti from the baking sheet.
Cool completely on the wire rack. Drizzle with
melted white or semi-sweet chocolate, if desired. Let
stand on a wax paper-lined tray until the chocolate
is firm. Store in a tightly covered container.

Makes about 3 dozen biscotti

COFFEE HOUSE INSPIRATION

**Present your desserts like a pro by drizzling
the desserts or dessert plates with lines of
melted chocolate. See our easy technique
on page 20.**

coffee date nut bread

Make this traditional quick bread extra-easy with a mix. Serve with
Coffee Maple Butter (recipe follows).

Prep: 10 minutes • Bake: 45 minutes

1 package (22 ounces) date quick bread mix
1 cup cold brewed double-strength coffee
1 cup toasted chopped walnuts

◆ **PREPARE** the bread mix according to package directions, substituting the coffee for the water. Gently stir in the nuts.

◆ **BAKE** and cool as directed. Cut into slices to serve.

Wrap in plastic wrap to store.

Makes 12 servings

COFFEE HOUSE TIP

For easier slicing, wrap the cooled bread in plastic wrap and store overnight.

coffee maple butter

Use this flavorful spread on muffins, toast, pancakes, or waffles.

Prep: 5 minutes

2 teaspoons instant coffee
½ teaspoon water
2 tablespoons maple-flavored syrup
½ cup butter *or* margarine, softened

◆ **STIR** the instant coffee and water in a small bowl until well blended. Stir in the syrup. Beat the butter in a large bowl with an electric mixer set on medium speed until light and fluffy. Gradually beat in the coffee mixture until blended.

◆ **REFRIGERATE** until ready to serve.

Makes about ⅔ cup

spiced orange coffee

You can serve this delicately scented coffee hot or cold.

Prep: 5 minutes

½ cup ground coffee

1 tablespoon grated orange peel

½ teaspoon ground cinnamon

⅓ cup firmly packed brown sugar

6 cups cold water

Cinnamon sticks and halved orange
  slices (optional)

✦ **PLACE** the coffee, orange peel, and cinnamon in the filter in the brew basket of a coffee maker. Place the brown sugar in the empty pot of the coffee maker.

✦ **PREPARE** the coffee with the cold water. When the brewing is complete, stir until well mixed. Pour into large cups or mugs. Serve with cinnamon sticks and halved orange slices, if desired.

Makes 8 servings

mocha punch

*This coffee ice cream punch will serve a crowd at brunches, showers,
or other get-togethers.*

Prep: 10 minutes

1 cup instant coffee

2 cups cold water

½ gallon (8 cups) coffee, vanilla, *or* chocolate
  ice cream, softened

1 quart milk

1 cup chocolate syrup

1 bottle (28 ounces) club soda, chilled

Additional ice cream (optional)

✦ **STIR** the instant coffee and water in a large bowl until well blended. Whisk in the ice cream, milk, chocolate syrup, and club soda. Serve immediately. Top each serving with small scoops of ice cream, if desired.

Makes about 30 servings

sour cream
streusel coffee cake

Sour cream adds moistness to a coffee cake that is layered with
a nutty brown-sugar streusel mixture.

Prep: 15 minutes • Bake: 50 minutes

3 tablespoons instant coffee, divided

2 tablespoons water

1 ¾ cups all-purpose flour

2 teaspoons baking powder

1 teaspoon baking soda

½ teaspoon salt

½ cup (1 stick) **butter** *or* **margarine,** at room
    temperature

1 cup granulated sugar

2 large eggs

1 cup sour cream

⅓ cup firmly packed brown sugar

⅓ cup toasted chopped **hazelnuts** *or* **walnuts**

¼ teaspoon ground cinnamon

✦ **HEAT** the oven to 350°F. Lightly butter a 9-inch tube
pan.

✦ **STIR** 2 tablespoons of the instant coffee and the
water in a small bowl until well blended; set aside.
Mix the flour, baking powder, baking soda, and salt
in a medium bowl; set aside.

✦ **BEAT** the butter and granulated sugar in a large bowl
with an electric mixer set on medium speed until
light and fluffy. Add the eggs, 1 at a time, beating
well after each addition. Stir in the coffee
mixture. Add the flour mixture alternately with the
sour cream, beating well after each addition until
smooth. Mix the brown sugar, the remaining 1
tablespoon of instant coffee, nuts, and cinnamon in
a small bowl. Spoon three-fourths of the batter into
the prepared pan; sprinkle with half of the brown
sugar mixture. Spoon the remaining batter on top;
sprinkle with the remaining brown sugar mixture.

✦ **BAKE** for 50 minutes or until a toothpick inserted
in the center comes out clean. Cool in the pan for
15 minutes on a wire rack. Loosen the cake from the
sides of the pan with a spatula or a knife. Gently
invert the cake onto the wire rack. Cool completely.
Cut into slices to serve.

Makes 10 to 12 servings

sour cream streusel coffee cake and
coffee maple butter (page 32)

carrot cake

Here's a different twist on a classic cake. Spicy and enhanced with coffee, this cake tastes especially good with a generous amount of Coffee Cream Cheese Frosting (recipe follows).

Prep: 20 minutes • Bake: 1 hour

2 cups all-purpose flour

2 cups granulated sugar

2 teaspoons baking soda

1 teaspoon baking powder

1 teaspoon salt

1 teaspoon ground cinnamon

½ teaspoon ground allspice

4 large eggs

2 tablespoons instant coffee

4 cups finely grated carrots

1 cup oil

1 cup chopped pecans

Coffee Cream Cheese Frosting (see following recipe)

✦ **HEAT** the oven to 350°F. Lightly butter and flour a 13x9-inch baking pan.

✦ **MIX** the flour, sugar, baking soda, baking powder, salt, and spices in a large bowl; set aside.

✦ **BEAT** the eggs and instant coffee in a large bowl with an electric mixer set on medium speed until well blended. Add the flour mixture, carrots, and oil and beat for 2 minutes on low speed until well blended. Stir in the nuts. Pour the mixture into the prepared pan.

✦ **BAKE** for 1 hour or until a toothpick inserted in the center comes out clean. Cool in the pan for 10 minutes on a wire rack. Loosen the cake from the sides of the pan with a spatula or a knife. Gently invert the cake onto the rack. Cool completely. Frost with Coffee Cream Cheese Frosting.

Makes 18 servings

coffee cream cheese frosting

Cream cheese adds an intriguingly tangy note to this velvety frosting.

Prep: 10 minutes

1 tablespoon instant coffee
1 tablespoon hot water
1 package (8 ounces) cream cheese, softened
4 ½ cups powdered sugar

+ **STIR** the instant coffee and hot water in a small bowl until well blended; set aside.

+ **BEAT** the cream cheese in a large bowl with an electric mixer set on medium speed until light and fluffy. Gradually beat in the powdered sugar until well blended. Beat in the coffee mixture until well blended.

Makes about 2 cups of frosting *or* enough to frost one 13x9-inch cake

coffee angel food cake

Using brewed coffee to prepare a packaged mix gives angel food cake a whole new taste.

Prep: 20 minutes • Bake: as directed on the package

1 package (16 ounces) angel food cake mix
Cold brewed strong coffee
Coffee Ice Cream (page 195)
Mexican Chocolate Sauce (page 195)
Whipped cream (optional)

+ **PREPARE** the cake mix as directed on the package for a 10-inch tube pan, substituting the brewed coffee for the water.

+ **BAKE** and cool as directed on the package. Serve the cake with Coffee Ice Cream, Mexican Chocolate Sauce, and whipped cream, if desired.

Makes 12 servings

coffee angel pie

A chewy meringue shell holds a heavenly coffee-flavored whipped cream mixture.
Topped with fresh fruit, this pie would be a spectacular addition to any brunch buffet.

Prep: 20 minutes • Bake: 30 minutes

MERINGUE SHELL:

2 egg whites, at room temperature

1 tablespoon instant coffee (optional)

¼ teaspoon cream of tartar

Dash of salt

⅔ cup granulated sugar

½ teaspoon vanilla extract

COFFEE WHIPPED CREAM:

1 cup heavy (whipping) cream

2 tablespoons granulated sugar

1 to 2 teaspoons instant coffee

½ teaspoon vanilla extract

Assorted fruit, for garnish (optional)

PREPARE THE MERINGUE SHELL:

✦ **HEAT** the oven to 325°F. Lightly butter a 9-inch pie plate.

✦ **BEAT** the egg whites, instant coffee, cream of tartar, and salt in a large bowl with an electric mixer set on high speed until foamy. Add the sugar, 2 tablespoons at a time, beating well after each addition. Continue beating until the mixture stands in stiff peaks. Gently fold in the vanilla. Spread the mixture on the bottom and side of the prepared pie plate, using the back of a spoon.

✦ **BAKE** for 30 minutes or until the shell feels dry and firm. Cool completely on a wire rack.

Makes 1 meringue shell

PREPARE THE COFFEE WHIPPED CREAM:

✦ **BEAT** the cream, sugar, instant coffee, and vanilla in a chilled large bowl with an electric mixer set on high speed until the cream holds its shape. (Do not overbeat.)

✦ **REFRIGERATE** until ready to serve. Just before serving, spoon the whipped cream into the meringue shell. Top with the assorted fruit, if desired. Cut into slices to serve

Makes 8 servings

COFFEE HOUSE INSPIRATION

Omit the meringue. Spoon the *coffee whipped cream* into stemmed dessert or wine glasses. Decorate with chocolate-covered coffee beans or chocolate curls for an easy, yet elegant dessert.

coffee angel pie

chocolate
nut loaves

Dark and delicious, these nutty loaves are great for gift-giving.

Prep: 20 minutes • Bake: 50 minutes

5 large eggs

3 tablespoons instant coffee

2 teaspoons vanilla extract

2 ¼ cups all-purpose flour

1 teaspoon baking soda

¼ teaspoon salt

1 cup (2 sticks) butter *or* margarine, softened

2 cups granulated sugar

3 squares (3 ounces) unsweetened chocolate,
   melted, cooled slightly

1 cup buttermilk

½ cup dried cherries

½ cup finely chopped nuts

Powdered sugar for sprinkling on the loaves
   (optional)

✦ **HEAT** the oven to 350°F. Lightly butter and flour
   five 5x3-inch loaf pans.

✦ **STIR** the eggs, instant coffee, and vanilla in a small
   bowl until well blended; set aside. Mix the flour,
   baking soda, and salt in a large bowl; set aside.

✦ **BEAT** the butter and sugar in a large bowl with an
   electric mixer set on medium speed until light and
   fluffy. Beat in the egg mixture. Stir in the chocolate.
   Add the flour mixture alternately with the buttermilk,
   beating after each addition until smooth. Mix in
   the cherries and nuts. Divide evenly among the
   prepared pans.

✦ **BAKE** for about 50 minutes or until a toothpick
   inserted in the centers of the loaves comes out
   clean. Cool the loaves in the pans for 10 minutes on
   wire racks. Loosen the loaves from the pans and
   remove them to the racks to cool completely. Sprinkle
   with powdered sugar, if desired. Cut into slices to
   serve. Wrap in plastic wrap to store.

Makes 5 loaves

COFFEE HOUSE TIP

**For easier slicing, wrap the cooled breads
in plastic wrap and store overnight.**

spiced apple
coffee cake

Moist and spicy, here's a coffee cake fit for welcoming a newcomer to the neighborhood.

Prep: 20 minutes • Bake: 60 minutes

2 cups all-purpose flour

1½ cups granulated sugar

2 teaspoons ground cinnamon

1 teaspoon baking soda

½ teaspoon salt

2 large eggs

½ cup oil

½ cup room temperature brewed strong coffee

2 teaspoons vanilla extract

2½ cups chopped peeled apples

1 cup chopped nuts

✦ **HEAT** the oven to 350°F. Lightly butter and flour a 9x5-inch loaf pan.

✦ **STIR** the flour, sugar, cinnamon, baking soda, and salt in a large bowl. Beat the eggs in a small bowl; stir in the oil, coffee, and vanilla. Add the egg mixture to the flour mixture and stir just until moistened. Stir in the apples and nuts. Pour the batter into the prepared pan.

✦ **BAKE** for 55 to 60 minutes or until a toothpick inserted in the center comes out clean. Cool in the pan for 10 minutes on a wire rack. Loosen the cake from the sides of the pan with a spatula or a knife. Gently invert the cake onto the wire rack. Cool completely. Cut into slices to serve.

Makes 12 servings

shortcakes with
espresso cream

*Ladyfingers, an Italian-style ricotta mixture, and fresh fruit create
an elegant plated dessert perfectly suited to a summer brunch.*

Prep: 15 minutes plus refrigeration time

1 container (15 ounces) whole milk
    ricotta cheese

²/₃ cup powdered sugar

¹/₈ to ¹/₄ teaspoon ground cinnamon

1 to 2 tablespoons instant coffee

1 teaspoon vanilla extract

1 cup heavy (whipping) cream

3 cups assorted sweetened fresh fruit, such as
    sliced strawberries, peaches,
    blueberries, *or* raspberries

2 packages (3 ounces each) ladyfingers,
    split into 3-finger segments

Powdered sugar for sprinkling over the dessert

Mint sprigs, for garnish (optional)

✦ **PLACE** the ricotta cheese, ²/₃ cup of powdered sugar, and cinnamon in a food processor container fitted with the steel blade; cover. Process until smooth. Spoon the mixture into a medium bowl.

✦ **STIR** the instant coffee and vanilla in a large bowl until well blended. Add the cream and beat with an electric mixer set on medium speed until soft peaks form. Gently stir the whipped cream mixture into the ricotta mixture.

✦ **REFRIGERATE** until ready to serve. For each serving, split each ladyfinger segment in half and place one half on a plate, cut-side facing up. Spoon the espresso cream and fruit over the segment. Cover with the top half segment, cut-side facing down. Sprinkle with powdered sugar. Garnish with mint sprigs, if desired. Serve immediately.

Makes 8 servings

easy coffee pound cake

Pound cake mix becomes much more interesting when it's made with coffee.

Prep: 15 minutes • Bake: as directed on the package

1 package (16 ounces) pound cake mix
Cold brewed strong coffee

+ **PREPARE** the cake mix as directed on the package for the 8x4-inch or 9x5-inch loaf pan, substituting the coffee for the water.

+ **BAKE** as directed. Cool in the pan for 10 minutes on a wire rack. Loosen the cake from the pan and remove it to the rack to cool completely. Cut into slices to serve.

Makes 8 servings

ENTERTAINING IDEA

Sunday is the perfect day to unwind before the beginning of the next week. Serve a main course such as an egg strata along with fruit salad, coffee and coffee drinks, and an assortment of coffee-flavored desserts.

For an easy ending to brunch, set up a dessert buffet. Toast slices of *easy coffee pound cake* and let your guests select the toppings: berries and sliced fresh fruit, scoops of ice cream, *hawaiian dessert sauce*, and *mocha sauce*. Serve with plenty of hot, freshly brewed coffee, or if the weather is warm, make some *iced coffee* (page 80) too.

hawaiian dessert sauce

Pineapple, coffee, and coconut are natural partners in this luscious sauce.

Prep: 10 minutes

⅓ cup granulated sugar

1 tablespoon cornstarch

½ cup water

1 can (8 ounces) crushed pineapple in juice, undrained

1 tablespoon butter *or* margarine

2 teaspoons instant coffee

¼ cup sweetened flaked coconut

¼ teaspoon vanilla extract

✦ **MIX** the sugar and cornstarch in a medium saucepan. Whisk in the water. Add the pineapple and the butter. Stirring constantly, cook over medium heat until the mixture comes to a boil, and boil for 1 minute. Remove the pan from the heat. Whisk in the instant coffee. Stir in the coconut and vanilla. Serve warm or chilled over ice cream, plain pudding, or pound cake. Store the leftover sauce in the refrigerator.

Makes about 1½ cups

mocha sauce

Serve this sauce warm over your favorite dessert or as a dip for fresh fruit.

Prep: 5 minutes • Microwave: 5 minutes

2 squares (2 ounces) unsweetened chocolate

⅓ cup water

½ cup granulated sugar

1 tablespoon instant coffee

3 tablespoons butter *or* margarine

¼ teaspoon vanilla extract

✦ **MICROWAVE** the chocolate and water in a large microwavable bowl on High for 1½ minutes. Stir until the chocolate is completely melted.

✦ **STIR** the sugar and instant coffee into the chocolate mixture. Microwave for 1 minute. Stir. Microwave for 2 minutes longer. Stir in the butter and vanilla. Serve warm over ice cream, pudding, or cake. Store the leftover sauce in the refrigerator. Reheat before serving.

Makes about 1 cup

coffee break

The coffee break is a typically American ritual—
fast, refreshing, and informal. The recipes in this chapter
are designed to fill the need for something good to eat,
like the *coffee fruit and nut bread* (page 55), or
toasted walnut biscotti (page 53),
when friends are invited home. You will be the
most popular person around if you bring to a meeting,
or any special gathering, a tray of your very own
coffee crunch kuchen (page 66).
A carafe of steaming *raspberry java* (page 65)
would be welcome, too.

chocolate chunk sour cream muffins

mocha chip rugalach

cappuccino sticky buns

almond macaroon coffee

cappuccino biscotti

toasted walnut biscotti

coffee fruit and nut bread

lemon ginger coffee

coffee cream cheese

mocha spice cake

coffee cake scones

cinnamon coffee crinkles

banana coffee cooler

coffee slushie

easy coffee cake

old-fashioned coffee pound cake

raspberry java

coffee crunch kuchen

coffee chunk streusel coffee cake

hot chocolate cappuccino

sugar 'n spice cappuccino

chocolate chunk
sour cream muffins

Moist coffee-flavored muffins, chock-full of chocolate chunks, are great to bring along to a morning get-together or an office meeting.

Prep: 15 minutes • Bake: 30 minutes

½ cup milk

2 tablespoons instant coffee

1½ cups all-purpose flour

½ cup granulated sugar

1½ teaspoons baking powder

½ teaspoon ground cinnamon

¼ teaspoon salt

2 large eggs

½ cup sour cream *or* plain yogurt

¼ cup (½ stick) butter *or* margarine, melted

1 teaspoon vanilla extract

1 package (4 ounces) German's sweet
   chocolate, chopped

✦ **HEAT** the oven to 375°F. Lightly butter 12 muffin pan cups (or line them with paper cups).

✦ **STIR** the milk and instant coffee in a small bowl until well blended; set aside.

✦ **STIR** the flour, sugar, baking powder, cinnamon, and salt in a large bowl. Beat the eggs in a medium bowl. Stir in the milk mixture, sour cream, butter, and vanilla until well blended. Add the egg mixture to the flour mixture and stir just until moistened. Stir in the chocolate. Spoon the batter into the prepared muffin cups, filling each cup two-thirds full.

✦ **BAKE** for 30 minutes or until a toothpick inserted in the center of one muffin comes out clean. Remove the pan to a wire rack and cool for 5 minutes. Remove the muffins from the pan and cool on the rack. Serve warm.

Makes 1 dozen muffins

mocha chip
rugalach

Vanilla ice cream is the secret ingredient that gives these rugalach their richness.

Prep: 30 minutes plus refrigeration time • Bake: 30 minutes

1 cup vanilla ice cream, slightly softened

2 tablespoons instant coffee

1 cup (2 sticks) butter *or* margarine, slightly softened

2 cups all-purpose flour

½ cup strawberry jam

1 cup semi-sweet chocolate chips

1 cup finely chopped nuts

Powdered sugar for sprinkling on the rugalach (optional)

◆ **HEAT** the oven to 350°F.

◆ **MIX** the ice cream and instant coffee in a small bowl until blended; set aside.

◆ **BEAT** the butter and flour in a large bowl with an electric mixer set on medium speed. Beat in the ice cream mixture. Divide the dough into 4 balls.

◆ **REFRIGERATE** for about 1 hour or until firm.

◆ **ROLL** out 1 ball at a time on a floured surface into a rectangle about ⅛ inch thick. Spread each rectangle evenly with 2 tablespoons of jam, sprinkle with ¼ cup chocolate chips, and ¼ cup nuts. Roll as for a jelly roll. Place the rolls on an ungreased baking sheet. Make 10 diagonal cuts in each roll, being careful not to cut all the way through.

◆ **BAKE** for 30 minutes or until golden brown. Remove the rugalach from the baking sheet and cool on a wire rack. Sprinkle with powdered sugar, if desired. Cut into slices to serve. Store in a tightly covered container.

Makes about 3½ dozen rugalach

A DROP OF HISTORY

1869   The Maxwell House, a hotel built by Colonel John Overton and named in honor of his wife, whose maiden name was Harriet Maxwell, is formally opened in Nashville. The hotel soon becomes famous for its fine cuisine.

cappuccino sticky buns

These gooey buns are a comforting treat to prepare on your next "snow day."
They can be made in a flash from ingredients you probably have on hand.

Prep: 10 minutes • Bake: 15 minutes

½ cup maple-flavored syrup
¼ cup (½ stick) butter *or* margarine
1 envelope instant cappuccino mix, any flavor
½ cup chopped pecans
1 can (7½ ounces) refrigerated biscuits

✦ **HEAT** the oven to 400°F.

✦ **STIR** the syrup and butter in a small saucepan. Bring the mixture just to a boil over medium heat.

✦ **STIR** in the cappuccino mix. Reduce the heat to low; cook and stir about 1 minute. Pour the mixture into an 8-inch round cake pan. Sprinkle with the pecans. Arrange the biscuits in the pan.

✦ **BAKE** for 12 to 15 minutes or until golden brown. Invert immediately onto a serving plate. Serve warm.

Makes 10 sticky buns

almond macaroon coffee

This coffee will remind you of the taste of nutty macaroons.

Prep: 5 minutes

½ cup ground coffee
⅓ cup granulated sugar
6 cups cold water
½ teaspoon almond extract

✦ **PLACE** the coffee in the filter in the brew basket of a coffee maker. Place the sugar in the empty pot of the coffee maker.

✦ **PREPARE** the coffee with the cold water. When the brewing is complete, stir in the almond extract. Pour into large cups or mugs.

Makes 8 servings

cappuccino sticky buns

cappuccino biscotti

Instant cappuccino mix adds a depth of flavor

that makes these cookies irresistible.

Prep: 20 minutes • Bake: 35 minutes

2 cups all-purpose flour

2 envelopes instant cappuccino mix, any flavor

1½ teaspoons baking powder

¼ teaspoon salt

½ cup (1 stick) butter *or* margarine, softened

¾ cup granulated sugar

2 large eggs

1 teaspoon vanilla extract

1 cup chopped nuts

✦ **HEAT** the oven to 325°F. Lightly butter and flour a large baking sheet.

✦ **MIX** the flour, cappuccino mixes, baking powder, and salt in a small bowl; set aside.

✦ **BEAT** the butter and sugar in a large bowl with an electric mixer set on medium speed until light and fluffy. Beat in the eggs and vanilla. Gradually add the flour mixture, beating well after each addition. Stir in the nuts.

✦ **DIVIDE** the dough into 2 equal portions. On a lightly floured surface, shape the dough into 2 logs, each 14 inches long, 1½ inches wide, and 1 inch thick. Place the logs 2 inches apart on the prepared baking sheet.

✦ **BAKE** for 25 minutes or until lightly browned. Set the baking sheet on a wire rack to cool for 10 minutes. Remove the logs from the baking sheet and place them on a cutting board. Using a serrated knife, cut each log diagonally into ¾-inch thick slices. Place the slices upright and ½ inch apart on the baking sheet. Bake for 10 minutes or until slightly dry. Remove the biscotti from the baking sheet. Cool completely on the wire rack. Store in a tightly covered container.

Makes about 3 dozen biscotti

COFFEE HOUSE INSPIRATION

For extra decadence, dip the cooled biscotti in melted chocolate. Melt 8 squares (8 ounces) of semi-sweet chocolate. Dip each of the biscotti halfway into the chocolate. Let the excess chocolate drip off. Place the biscotti on a wax paper-lined tray. Let stand at room temperature or refrigerate until the chocolate is firm.

toasted walnut biscotti

These crunchy cookies are a great idea for a mid-morning pick-me-up.

Prep: 15 minutes • Bake: 40 minutes

4 large eggs

2 tablespoons instant coffee

2 teaspoons vanilla extract

3 cups all-purpose flour

1 teaspoon baking powder

1 cup (2 sticks) butter *or* margarine, softened

1 cup granulated sugar

1 cup toasted chopped walnuts

✦ **HEAT** the oven to 350°F. Lightly butter and flour 2 large baking sheets.

✦ **STIR** the eggs, instant coffee, and vanilla in a small bowl until well blended; set aside. Mix the flour and baking powder in a medium bowl; set aside.

✦ **BEAT** the butter and sugar in a large bowl with an electric mixer set on medium speed until light and fluffy. Beat in the egg mixture. Gradually add the flour mixture, beating well after each addition. Stir in the walnuts.

✦ **DIVIDE** the dough into 2 equal portions. On a lightly floured surface, shape the dough into 4 logs, each 10 inches long, 2½ inches wide, and ¾ inch thick. Place the logs 2 inches apart on the prepared baking sheets.

✦ **BAKE** for 25 minutes or until lightly browned. Set the baking sheet on a wire rack to cool for 10 minutes. Remove the logs from the baking sheets and place on a cutting board. Using a serrated knife, cut each log diagonally into ¾-inch thick slices. Place the slices upright and ½-inch apart on the baking sheets. Bake for 10 to 15 minutes or until slightly dry. Remove the biscotti from the baking sheets. Cool completely on the wire rack. Store in a tightly covered container.

Makes about 5 dozen biscotti

COFFEE HOUSE TIP

Toasting nuts adds a deeper flavor and a crunchy texture to the nuts. Spread the nuts in a shallow pan. Toast at 400°F for 8 to 10 minutes or until golden, stirring frequently. Not only are toasted nuts great in baked goods, they are also superb when sprinkled on top of ice cream or other desserts.

coffee fruit and nut bread

This home-baked loaf will keep you coming back for "just one more slice."

Prep: 15 minutes • Bake: 1 hour

1 cup buttermilk

2 tablespoons instant coffee

5 cups all-purpose flour

1 cup plus 2 tablespoons granulated sugar, divided

4 teaspoons baking powder

½ teaspoon baking soda

½ teaspoon salt

3 large eggs

1 cup sour cream

1 cup coarsely chopped nuts

½ cup dried cranberries

½ cup golden raisins

1 tablespoon butter

✦ **HEAT** the oven to 350°F. Lightly butter a large baking sheet.

✦ **STIR** the buttermilk and instant coffee in a medium bowl until well blended; set aside.

✦ **MIX** the flour, 1 cup of the sugar, the baking powder, baking soda, and salt in a large bowl. Stir in the buttermilk mixture, sour cream, and eggs until a stiff dough forms. Stir in the nuts and dried fruits. Shape the dough into an 8-inch round loaf on the prepared baking sheet. Cut an "X" on the surface and top with the butter. Sprinkle evenly with the remaining 2 tablespoons of sugar.

✦ **BAKE** for 1 hour or until a toothpick inserted in the center comes out clean. Remove the bread from the baking sheet and cool on a wire rack. Cut into slices to serve. Wrap in plastic wrap to store.

Makes 1 large loaf

coffee fruit and nut bread

lemon ginger coffee

You can add drama to this coffee by serving it with a jaunty swirl of lemon peel dangling over the edge of each cup.

Prep: 5 minutes

6 tablespoons ground coffee
1 tablespoon grated lemon peel
½ teaspoon ground ginger
⅓ cup honey
4½ cups cold water

✦ **PLACE** the coffee, lemon peel, and ginger in the filter in the brew basket of a coffee maker. Pour the honey into the empty pot of the coffee maker.

✦ **PREPARE** the coffee with the cold water. When the brewing is complete, stir until well mixed. Pour into large cups or mugs.

Makes 6 servings

coffee cream cheese

Coffee lovers will especially enjoy this spread with their morning bagels.

Prep: 5 minutes

1 tablespoon milk
1 teaspoon instant coffee
1 package (8 ounces) cream cheese, softened
3 tablespoons powdered sugar

✦ **STIR** the milk and instant coffee in a small bowl until well blended. Beat in the cream cheese until smooth. Stir in the powdered sugar until well blended.

✦ **REFRIGERATE** until ready to serve.

Makes about 1 cup

COFFEE HOUSE TIP

You can soften cream cheese quickly in the microwave. Place 1 completely unwrapped package of cream cheese in a microwavable bowl. Microwave on High for 15 seconds.

mocha spice cake

Spice cake enhanced with coffee and chocolate is a sure winner.

Prep: 20 minutes • Bake: 45 minutes

1 container (8 ounces) sour cream

½ cup room temperature brewed double-strength coffee

½ teaspoon vanilla extract

2 squares (2 ounces) unsweetened chocolate

½ cup (1 stick) butter *or* margarine

1½ cups granulated sugar

2 large eggs

1½ cups all-purpose flour, divided

1 teaspoon baking soda

1 teaspoon ground cinnamon

½ teaspoon baking powder

½ teaspoon salt

Powdered sugar for sprinkling over the spice cake (optional)

✦ **HEAT** the oven to 325°F. Butter and flour a 13 x 9-inch baking pan.

✦ **STIR** the sour cream, coffee, and vanilla extract in a small bowl until well blended; set aside.

✦ **MICROWAVE** the chocolate and butter in a large microwavable bowl on High for 2 minutes or until the butter is melted. Stir until the chocolate is completely melted. Stir the sugar into the melted chocolate until well blended.

✦ **BEAT** in the eggs, 1 at a time, with an electric mixer set on low speed, beating well after each addition. Beat in ½ cup of the flour, baking soda, cinnamon, baking powder, and salt. Add the remaining flour alternately with the sour cream mixture, beating thoroughly after each addition until smooth. Pour the mixture into the prepared pan.

✦ **BAKE** for 45 minutes or until a toothpick inserted in the center of the cake comes out clean. Cool completely on a wire rack. Sprinkle with powdered sugar, if desired. Cut into squares to serve.

Makes 15 to 18 servings

COFFEE HOUSE TIP

This cake can also be baked in a buttered and floured 9-inch tube pan. The baking time will be 1 hour. Cool the cake in the pan for 10 minutes before removing it from the pan to a wire rack to cool completely.

coffee cake
scones

Here's a homemade treat that combines the best features of both scones and coffee cake.

Prep: 20 minutes • Bake: 14 minutes

SCONES:

2 cups all-purpose flour

½ cup granulated sugar

2 teaspoons baking powder

¼ teaspoon salt

½ cup (1 stick) butter *or* margarine, chilled

2 large eggs

⅓ cup heavy (whipping) cream

2 tablespoons instant coffee

¼ teaspoon vanilla extract

BROWN SUGAR CINNAMON TOPPING:

¼ cup all-purpose flour

2 tablespoons firmly packed brown sugar

⅛ teaspoon ground cinnamon

2 tablespoons butter *or* margarine

Powdered sugar for sprinkling on top of the scones (optional)

Fresh fruit and mint sprigs, for garnish (optional)

PREPARE THE SCONES:

✦ **HEAT** the oven to 425°F. Lightly butter and flour a large baking sheet.

✦ **MIX** the flour, sugar, baking powder, and salt in a large bowl. Using a pastry blender or 2 knives, cut in the butter until the mixture resembles coarse crumbs. Beat the eggs in a medium bowl. Stir in the cream, instant coffee, and vanilla until well blended. Add to the flour mixture and stir until a soft dough forms. Shape the dough into a ball. With lightly floured hands, pat the dough into an 8- to 9-inch circle on the prepared baking sheet.

PREPARE THE BROWN SUGAR CINNAMON TOPPING:

✦ **MIX** the flour, brown sugar, and cinnamon in a small bowl. Using a pastry blender or 2 knives, cut in the butter until the mixture resembles coarse crumbs. Sprinkle the topping mixture on the scone dough. With a serrated knife, cut the circle into 8 wedges, being careful not to cut all the way through.

✦ **BAKE** for 12 to 14 minutes or until a toothpick inserted in the center comes out clean. Sprinkle the scones with powdered sugar, if desired. Garnish with fresh fruit and mint sprigs, if desired. Serve warm. Cut into wedges to serve.

Makes 8 scones

coffee cake scones

cinnamon coffee
crinkles

These cinnamon-spiced cookies are perfect with
any coffee drink.

Prep: 15 minutes • Bake: 12 minutes

2 large eggs

2 tablespoons instant coffee

2¾ cups all-purpose flour

2 teaspoons cream of tartar

1 teaspoon baking soda

1 teaspoon ground cinnamon

¼ teaspoon salt

½ cup (1 stick) butter *or* margarine, softened

½ cup shortening

1½ cups granulated sugar

Powdered sugar for coating the cookies

♦ **HEAT** the oven to 400°F.

♦ **STIR** the eggs and instant coffee in a small bowl until well blended; set aside. Mix the flour, cream of tartar, baking soda, cinnamon, and salt in a medium bowl; set aside.

♦ **BEAT** the butter, shortening, granulated sugar, and egg mixture in a large bowl with an electric mixer set on medium speed until light and fluffy. Stir in the flour mixture. Shape the dough into 1-inch balls. Roll the balls in the powdered sugar. Place 2 inches apart on ungreased baking sheets.

♦ **BAKE** for 10 to 12 minutes or until set. Remove the cookies from the baking sheets. Cool completely on wire racks. Store in a tightly covered container.

Makes about 4 dozen cookies

banana coffee cooler

A delicious and grown-up milkshake.

Prep: 10 minutes

1 cup cold brewed double-strength coffee

1 large ripe banana, sliced

1 pint coffee *or* vanilla ice cream (2 cups), softened

✦ **PLACE** the coffee and banana in a blender container; cover. Blend on high speed until smooth. Add the ice cream; cover. Blend until smooth. Pour into tall glasses. Serve immediately.

Makes 4 servings

coffee slushie

Coffee ice cubes add an extra hit of coffee to this ice cream beverage.

Prep: 5 minutes

½ cup cold brewed double-strength coffee

8 Coffee Ice Cubes (page 97)

½ cup coffee, chocolate, *or* vanilla ice cream, softened

✦ **PLACE** all the ingredients in a blender container; cover. Blend on high speed until the ice cubes are crushed. Pour into tall glasses. Serve immediately.

Makes 2 servings

easy coffee cake

Using a buttermilk baking mix makes this recipe extra simple to prepare.

Prep: 10 minutes • Bake: 22 minutes

2 ⅓ cups buttermilk baking mix, divided

⅔ cup firmly packed brown sugar, divided

½ teaspoon ground cinnamon

2 tablespoons butter *or* margarine

½ cup cold brewed double-strength coffee

¼ cup milk

1 large egg

Powdered sugar for sprinkling on top of the
    coffee cake (optional)

+ **HEAT** the oven to 375°F. Lightly butter a 9-inch
    round cake pan.

+ **MIX** ⅓ cup of the baking mix, ⅓ cup of brown
    sugar, and the cinnamon in a medium bowl. Using
    a pastry blender or 2 knives, cut in the butter until
    the mixture resembles coarse crumbs; set aside.

+ **STIR** the remaining 2 cups of baking mix, the
    remaining ⅓ cup of brown sugar, the coffee, milk,
    and egg in a medium bowl until well blended.
    Pour the batter into the prepared pan. Sprinkle
    with the cinnamon mixture.

+ **BAKE** for 18 to 22 minutes or until golden brown.
    Cool the cake in the pan for 10 minutes. Remove
    the cake from the pan and cool on a wire rack. Cut
    into slices to serve.

Makes 10 servings

COFFEE HOUSE INSPIRATION

**To create a lattice design on top of the
cake: Cut 1-inch strips of wax paper and
place them on top of the cake, leaving
about ½-inch between the strips. Sprinkle
with powdered sugar to create parallel
stripes. Carefully remove the wax paper
strips and arrange them perpendicular to
the stripes, again about ½-inch apart.
Sprinkle again with powdered sugar and
carefully remove the strips.**

easy coffee cake

old-fashioned coffee pound cake

This is the real thing—full of buttery richness!

Prep: 20 minutes • Bake: 1½ hours

4 cups all-purpose flour

1½ teaspoons baking powder

1 teaspoon ground cinnamon

1 teaspoon salt

2 cups (4 sticks) butter *or* margarine

2½ cups granulated sugar

7 large eggs

1 cup room temperature brewed double-strength coffee

Powdered sugar for sprinkling over the pound cake (optional)

✦ **HEAT** the oven to 350°F. Butter a 10-inch tube pan.

✦ **MIX** the flour, baking powder, cinnamon, and salt in a medium bowl; set aside.

✦ **BEAT** the butter and granulated sugar in a large bowl with an electric mixer set on medium speed until light and fluffy. Add the eggs, 1 at a time, beating well after each addition. Add the flour mixture alternately in thirds with the coffee, beating after each addition until smooth. Pour the batter into the prepared pan.

✦ **BAKE** 1½ hours or until a toothpick inserted near the center of the cake comes out clean. Remove the pan to a wire rack and cool for 10 minutes. Loosen the cake from the sides of the pan with a spatula or a knife and gently remove the cake. Cool completely on the rack. Sprinkle the cake with powdered sugar, if desired. Cut into slices to serve.

Makes 16 servings

raspberry java

Raspberry jam gives this coffee a fruity sweetness. For an attractive presentation, decorate each cup with rosy fresh raspberries threaded onto a toothpick.

Prep: 5 minutes

6 tablespoons ground coffee

3 tablespoons raspberry jam

4½ cups cold water

Fresh raspberries, for garnish (optional)

+ **PLACE** the coffee in the filter in the brew basket of a coffee maker. Spoon the jam into the empty pot of the coffee maker.

+ **PREPARE** the coffee with the cold water. When the brewing is complete, stir until well mixed. Pour into large cups or mugs. Garnish each serving with 3 raspberries on a toothpick, if desired.

Makes 6 servings

COFFEE HOUSE INSPIRATION

A light dusting of powdered sugar or cocoa powder can add a special look to the top of any dessert. Desserts and beverages topped with whipped cream or whipped topping look especially nice sprinkled with cocoa powder. Place about 1 tablespoon of the powdered sugar or cocoa powder inside a small, fine-meshed strainer. Hold the handle in one hand and gently tap the side of the strainer with the other hand to delicately sprinkle the powdered sugar or cocoa powder over the surface.

coffee crunch
kuchen

This kuchen is a homey recipe that has a rich brown sugar flavor.
A drizzling of white chocolate adds extra appeal.

Prep: 15 minutes • Bake: 35 minutes

2¼ cups all-purpose flour

2 cups firmly packed brown sugar

1 tablespoon baking powder

1 cup (2 sticks) butter *or* margarine

½ cup chopped pecans

1 teaspoon ground cinnamon

2 large eggs

½ cup room temperature brewed strong coffee

½ cup evaporated milk

Melted white chocolate for drizzling on top of
the kuchen (optional)

✦ **HEAT** the oven to 375°F. Lightly butter and flour
a 13x9-inch baking pan.

✦ **MIX** the flour, brown sugar, and baking powder in
a large bowl. With a pastry blender or 2 knives, cut
in the butter until the mixture resembles coarse
crumbs. Stir in the pecans. Mix the cinnamon and
1 cup of the flour mixture in a small bowl; set
aside.

✦ **BEAT** the eggs in a medium bowl with an electric
mixer set on medium speed. Mix in the coffee and
milk. Stir in the remaining flour mixture just until
moistened. Pour the batter into the prepared pan.
Sprinkle evenly with the reserved cinnamon
mixture.

✦ **BAKE** for 30 to 35 minutes or until a toothpick
inserted in the center comes out clean. Drizzle
with melted white chocolate, if desired. Serve
warm.

Makes 12 to 15 servings

COFFEE HOUSE INSPIRATIONS

**Add an interesting shape to this coffee treat.
Use a round cookie cutter to cut the kuchen
into circles or use a knife to cut it into
triangles.**

**Drizzling desserts or dessert plates with thin
lines of melted chocolate can help you
present your desserts like a pro. See our
easy technique on page 20.**

coffee crunch kuchen with raspberry java (page 65)

chocolate chunk
streusel coffee cake

Streusel and melted chunks of chocolate—who could ask for anything more?
This yummy coffee cake would be a hit at your next brunch
or you could pack a square in a lunch bag.

Prep: 15 minutes • Bake: 25 minutes

⅔ cup all-purpose flour

½ cup firmly packed brown sugar

¼ cup (½ stick) butter *or* margarine

6 squares (6 ounces) semi-sweet chocolate,
  chopped, divided

⅓ cup chopped slivered almonds

1 package (2-layer size) yellow cake mix

Cold brewed double-strength coffee

◆ **HEAT** the oven to 350°F. Lightly butter a
15x10x1-inch baking pan.

◆ **MIX** the flour and brown sugar in a medium bowl.
Using a pastry blender or 2 knives, cut in the butter until the mixture resembles coarse crumbs. Stir
in half of the chopped chocolate and the almonds.

◆ **PREPARE** the cake mix as directed on the
package, substituting the brewed coffee for
the water. Pour the batter into the prepared pan.
Sprinkle with the streusel mixture and the
remaining chopped chocolate.

◆ **BAKE** for 20 to 25 minutes or until a toothpick
inserted in the center comes out clean. Cool on a
wire rack. Cut into squares to serve.

Makes 24 servings

COFFEE HOUSE INSPIRATION

**A chocolate-dipped cinnamon stick is a fla-
vorful stirrer for a cup of coffee or cappuccino. Melt at least 4 squares (4 ounces) of
semi-sweet chocolate, bittersweet chocolate,
or white chocolate. Dip cinnamon sticks
halfway into the chocolate and let the excess
chocolate drip off. Let stand at room
temperature or refrigerate on a wax paper-
lined tray for 30 minutes or until the
chocolate is firm.**

hot chocolate
cappuccino

Melted chocolate makes this popular beverage a special treat.

Prep: 5 minutes

1 cup milk

1 square (1 ounce) semi-sweet *or* white
   chocolate, chopped

1 envelope instant cappuccino mix, any flavor

✦ **MICROWAVE** the milk and chocolate in a
medium microwavable bowl on High for 1 minute.
Stir until the chocolate is completely melted and
the mixture is smooth. Stir in the cappuccino mix.
Pour into a large cup or mug.

Makes 1 serving

sugar 'n spice
cappuccino

Try this favorite with a chocolate-dipped cinnamon stick (see preceding page).

Prep: 5 minutes

1 envelope instant cappuccino mix, any flavor

1 cup hot milk

1 teaspoon brown sugar

Cinnamon stick

✦ **PREPARE** the cappuccino mix as directed on
the package, substituting the 1 cup of hot milk
for the hot water. Add the brown sugar and stir
with the cinnamon stick.

Makes 1 serving

lunch

Lunch becomes a special occasion when you offer
a homemade dessert. For a more formal meal, serve the
café latte cheesecake with or without the
easy coffee caramel sauce (page 94).
For something more casual, try the *banana split
cheesecake squares* on page 91.
You'll also find plenty of terrific cookie and
brownie recipes that travel well and will be eagerly
received at any time and any place by everyone.
And we've included some tips on how to store
leftovers — should there be any.

triple mocha brownies
double cappuccino brownies
coffee cinnamon cream cheese brownies
banana caramel café pie
cappuccino yogurt muffins
tropical coffee banana bread
iced coffee
chocolate chunk coffee cookies
cranberry macadamia jumbles
white chocolate ginger biscotti
cinnamon mocha squares
café au lait parfaits
fluffy coffee cheesecake
raspberry sauce
coffee smoothie
coffee soda
banana split cheesecake squares
sugar & spice coffee
orange cappuccino float
thai coffee
mocha orange coffee
café latte cheesecake
easy coffee caramel sauce
easy mocha cookies
coffee milk
coffee ice cubes

triple mocha brownies

These rich brownies deliver a triple coffee hit.

Prep: 20 minutes • Bake: 45 minutes

BROWNIE:

¾ cup (1½ sticks) butter *or* margarine

4 squares (4 ounces) unsweetened chocolate

2 cups granulated sugar

4 large eggs

2 tablespoons instant coffee

1 teaspoon vanilla extract

1 cup all-purpose flour

CRUNCH TOPPING:

¼ cup (½ stick) butter *or* margarine

½ cup firmly packed brown sugar

1 large egg

1 tablespoon instant coffee

1 teaspoon vanilla extract

6 squares (6 ounces) semi-sweet chocolate, coarsely chopped

1 cup coarsely chopped walnuts

MOCHA DRIZZLE:

2 squares (2 ounces) semi-sweet chocolate

1 tablespoon butter *or* margarine

¼ teaspoon instant coffee

PREPARE THE BROWNIES:

✦ **HEAT** the oven to 350°F. Line a 13x9-inch baking pan with foil; lightly butter the foil.

✦ **MICROWAVE** the butter and chocolate in a large microwavable bowl on High for 2 minutes or until the butter has melted. Stir until the chocolate is completely melted.

✦ **STIR** the granulated sugar, eggs, instant coffee, and vanilla into the melted chocolate until well blended. Stir in the flour until well blended. Spread the batter in the prepared pan.

✦ **BAKE** for 25 minutes. Place the pan on a wire rack.

PREPARE THE CRUNCH TOPPING:

✦ **MICROWAVE** the butter and brown sugar in a small bowl on High for 1 minute or until the butter has melted. Mix in the egg, instant coffee, and vanilla until well blended. Stir in the chopped chocolate and walnuts. Spread over the brownies.

✦ **BAKE** for 20 minutes longer or until a toothpick inserted in the center comes out with fudgy crumbs. (Do not overbake.) Cool completely in the pan on a wire rack.

PREPARE THE MOCHA DRIZZLE:

✦ **MICROWAVE** the remaining chocolate, butter, and instant coffee in a small microwavable bowl on High for 1 minute or until the butter has melted. Stir until the chocolate is completely melted. Drizzle over the brownies. Let stand until the chocolate is firm. Cut into squares to serve. Store in a tightly covered container.

Makes 2 dozen brownies

double cappuccino
brownies

Cappuccino flavors both the brownie and the frosting.

Prep: 10 minutes • Bake: 35 minutes

¾ cup (1½ sticks) butter *or* margarine

4 squares (4 ounces) unsweetened chocolate

2 cups granulated sugar

4 large eggs

1 teaspoon vanilla extract

1 cup all-purpose flour

1 envelope instant cappuccino mix, any flavor

1 cup coarsely chopped nuts (optional)

Cappuccino Buttercream Frosting (page 144)

+ **HEAT** the oven to 350°F. Line a 13x9-inch baking pan with foil; lightly butter the foil.

+ **MICROWAVE** the butter and chocolate in a large microwavable bowl on High for 2 minutes or until the butter has melted. Stir until the chocolate is completely melted.

+ **STIR** the sugar into the chocolate mixture until well blended. Mix in the eggs and vanilla. Stir in the flour, cappuccino mix, and nuts until well blended. Spread the batter in the prepared pan.

+ **BAKE** for 30 to 35 minutes or until a toothpick inserted in the center comes out with fudgy crumbs. (Do not overbake.) Cool completely in the pan on a wire rack. Frost the brownies with Cappuccino Buttercream Frosting. Cut into squares to serve. Store in a tightly covered container.

Makes 2 dozen brownies

COFFEE HOUSE INSPIRATION

For a more sophisticated look, cut the brownies into diamonds or triangles instead of squares.

coffee cinnamon cream cheese brownies

Cinnamon-flavored cream cheese batter swirled over the top of these rich fudgy brownies makes them irresistible.

Prep: 15 minutes • Bake: 40 minutes

BROWNIE BOTTOM:

¾ cup (1½ sticks) butter *or* margarine

4 squares (4 ounces) unsweetened chocolate

2 cups granulated sugar

4 large eggs

3 tablespoons instant coffee

1 teaspoon vanilla extract

1¼ cups all-purpose flour

CREAM CHEESE TOPPING:

1 package (8 ounces) cream cheese, softened

⅓ cup granulated sugar

1 large egg

2 tablespoons all-purpose flour

½ teaspoon ground cinnamon

PREPARE THE BROWNIE BOTTOM:

✦ **HEAT** the oven to 350°F. Line a 13x9-inch baking pan with foil; lightly butter the foil.

✦ **MICROWAVE** the butter and chocolate in a large microwavable bowl on High for 2 minutes or until the butter has melted. Stir until the chocolate is completely melted.

✦ **STIR** the sugar into the chocolate mixture until well blended. Mix in the eggs, instant coffee, and vanilla. Stir in the flour until well blended. Spread the brownie batter in the prepared baking pan.

PREPARE THE CREAM CHEESE TOPPING:

✦ **BEAT** the cream cheese, sugar, egg, flour, and cinnamon in the same bowl until well blended. Spoon the mixture over the brownie batter. Swirl with a knife to marbleize.

✦ **BAKE** for 40 minutes or until a toothpick inserted in the center comes out with fudgy crumbs. (Do not overbake.) Cool completely in the pan on a wire rack. Cut into squares. Store the leftover brownies in the refrigerator.

Makes 2 dozen brownies

coffee cinnamon cream cheese brownies with double cappuccino brownies (page 73) and triple mocha brownies (page 72)

banana caramel
café pie

Can your friends and family identify the special ingredients

in this banana cream pie?

Prep: 10 minutes • Refrigerate: 3 hours

1 large ripe banana, sliced

1 prepared chocolate flavor crumb crust
   (6 ounces *or* 9 inches)

2 cups cold milk

1 tablespoon instant coffee

2 packages (4-serving size each) white
   chocolate *or* vanilla flavor instant pudding
   & pie filling

1 tub (8 ounces) frozen whipped topping,
   thawed, divided

Caramel dessert topping for spooning on the
   dessert plates and for garnish

✦ **ARRANGE** the banana slices in the bottom of the crust.

✦ **STIR** the milk and instant coffee in a medium bowl until well blended. Add the pudding mixes. Beat with a wire whisk for 1 minute. (The mixture will be thick.) Gently stir in half of the whipped topping. Spoon the pudding mixture into the crust, spreading evenly with the back of a spoon.

✦ **REFRIGERATE** for 3 hours or until firm. Cut the pie into 8 slices. Spoon the caramel topping onto 8 dessert plates. Place a slice of pie on each plate. Garnish with the remaining whipped topping and additional caramel topping, if desired. Store the leftover pie in the refrigerator.

Makes 8 servings

cappuccino yogurt
muffins

Here's a delightful mixture of flavors—sweet cappuccino and the tang of yogurt. Chopped dried apricots and toasted almonds contribute taste and texture. These muffins are winners.

Prep: 15 minutes • Bake: 30 minutes

1½ cups all-purpose flour

½ cup granulated sugar

1 envelope instant cappuccino mix, any flavor

1½ teaspoons baking powder

½ teaspoon ground cinnamon

¼ teaspoon salt

2 large eggs, lightly beaten

½ cup cold brewed strong coffee

½ cup coffee *or* vanilla flavor yogurt

¼ cup (½ stick) butter *or* margarine, melted

½ cup toasted chopped almonds

½ cup chopped dried apricots

+ **HEAT** the oven to 375°F. Lightly butter 12 muffin pan cups (or line them with paper cups).

+ **STIR** the flour, sugar, cappuccino mix, baking power, cinnamon, and salt in a large bowl. Stir the eggs, coffee, yogurt, and melted butter in a medium bowl until well blended. Add the egg mixture to the flour mixture and stir just until moistened. Stir in the almonds and apricots. Spoon the batter into the prepared muffin cups, filling each cup two-thirds full.

+ **BAKE** for 25 to 30 minutes or until a toothpick inserted in the center of one muffin comes out clean. Remove the pan to a wire rack and cool for 5 minutes. Remove the muffins from the pan and cool completely on the rack. Serve warm.

Makes 1 dozen muffins

COFFEE HOUSE TIP

There is nothing like the aroma of freshly baking muffins to add a cozy feeling to your home. Plan ahead to serve muffins warm from the oven. The day (or night) before, measure the flour and other dry ingredients into a mixing bowl. Chop and measure any "stir-ins" such as nuts or dried fruits. Cover with plastic wrap to store overnight. Shortly before you are ready to serve the muffins, preheat the oven and combine with the remaining ingredients.

tropical coffee
banana bread

An everyday quick bread mix becomes extraordinary when it is prepared with coffee and has crushed pineapple, coconut, and macadamia nuts added to it.

Prep: 10 minutes • Bake: 40 to 55 minutes

1 package (14 ounces) banana quick bread mix
½ cup cold brewed double-strength coffee
1 can (8 ounces) crushed pineapple, undrained
½ cup sweetened flaked coconut, toasted
½ cup chopped macadamia nuts

✦ **PREPARE** the mix according to the package directions, substituting the coffee for the water. Gently stir in the pineapple, coconut, and macadamia nuts.

✦ **BAKE** the bread and cool as directed. Cut into slices to serve. Wrap in plastic wrap and store in the refrigerator.

Makes 12 servings

COFFEE HOUSE TIPS

For easier slicing, wrap the cooled bread in plastic wrap and store overnight in the refrigerator.

To toast coconut, spread in a shallow pan. Toast at 350°F for 7 to 12 minutes or until lightly browned, stirring frequently.

tropical coffee banana bread

iced coffee

Use Coffee Ice Cubes (page 97) to chill your beverage and maintain its full coffee flavor.

Prep: 5 minutes

6 tablespoons ground coffee

3 cups cold water

Coffee Ice Cubes (page 97) *or* ice cubes

Milk and sugar, to taste (optional)

✦ **PREPARE** the coffee with the cold water in a coffee maker. Refrigerate until ready to serve. Pour the coffee over the ice cubes in tall glasses. Serve with milk and sugar, if desired.

Makes 4 servings

COFFEE HOUSE INSPIRATIONS

Cinnamon Iced Coffee: Add ½ teaspoon ground cinnamon to the ground coffee in the brew basket before brewing.

Iced Coffee Latte: Pour ⅓ cup cold brewed coffee into a large glass. Stir in ½ cup cold milk. Add ice cubes and sugar to taste, if desired.

A DROP OF HISTORY

1873 Joel Cheek's career in coffee begins when he moves to Nashville, Tennessee, and secures a position with a wholesale grocery firm as a salesman specializing in coffee.

chocolate chunk
coffee cookies

Chocolate chunk cookies take on a whole new dimension when they are flavored with coffee and cinnamon.

Prep: 10 minutes • Bake: 10 minutes

1 large egg

1 tablespoon instant coffee

1 teaspoon vanilla extract

8 squares (8 ounces) semi-sweet chocolate

½ cup (1 stick) butter *or* margarine, softened

½ cup granulated sugar

½ cup firmly packed brown sugar

1 cup all-purpose flour

1 cup quick-cooking oats

½ teaspoon baking soda

½ teaspoon ground cinnamon

½ cup chopped nuts

+ **HEAT** the oven to 375°F.

+ **STIR** the egg, instant coffee, and vanilla in a small bowl until blended; set aside. Break the chocolate squares in half; cut each half into 3 chunks.

+ **BEAT** the butter and sugars in a large bowl with an electric mixer set on medium speed until light and fluffy. Mix in the egg mixture. Beat in the flour, oats, baking soda, and cinnamon on low speed until well blended. Stir in the chocolate chunks and nuts. Drop the dough by rounded tablespoonfuls, 2 inches apart, onto ungreased baking sheets.

+ **BAKE** for 10 minutes or until lightly browned. Set the baking sheets on wire racks to cool for 2 minutes. Using a metal spatula, transfer the cookies to the wire racks. Cool completely. Store in a tightly covered container.

Makes about 2 dozen cookies

cranberry macadamia jumbles

Dried cranberries, macadamia nuts, and two kinds of chocolate—
surely a combination made in heaven!

Prep: 20 minutes • Bake: 12 minutes

1 large egg

2 tablespoons instant coffee

1 teaspoon vanilla extract

½ cup (1 stick) butter *or* margarine

½ cup granulated sugar

¼ cup firmly packed brown sugar

1 cup all-purpose flour

1 teaspoon baking soda

¼ teaspoon salt

3 squares (3 ounces) semi-sweet chocolate, chopped

3 squares (3 ounces) white chocolate, chopped

2 cups chopped macadamia nuts

1½ cups dried cranberries

✦ **HEAT** the oven to 350°F.

✦ **STIR** the egg, instant coffee, and vanilla in a small bowl until well blended; set aside.

✦ **BEAT** the butter and sugars in a large bowl with an electric mixer set on medium speed until light and fluffy. Mix in the egg mixture. Beat in the flour, baking soda, and salt on low speed until well blended. Stir in the chocolates, nuts, and cranberries. Drop the dough by rounded tablespoonfuls, 2 inches apart, onto ungreased baking sheets.

✦ **BAKE** for 10 to 12 minutes or until golden brown. Set the baking sheets on wire racks to cool for 2 to 3 minutes. Using a metal spatula, transfer the cookies to the wire racks. Cool completely. Store in a tightly covered container.

Makes about 3 dozen cookies

COFFEE HOUSE INSPIRATION

Substitute an equal amount of other varieties of chocolate, nuts, and dried fruits for the macadamia nuts and dried cranberries. For instance, white chocolate, chopped walnuts, and dried apricots make an especially delicious combination.

cranberry macadamia jumbles
with coffee milk (page 97)

white chocolate ginger biscotti

*Crystallized ginger and white chocolate
add stylish flair to these biscotti.*

Prep: 20 minutes • Bake: 35 minutes

2 large eggs

2 tablespoons instant coffee

1 teaspoon vanilla extract

2 cups all-purpose flour

1 1/2 teaspoons baking powder

1/4 teaspoon salt

1/2 cup (1 stick) butter *or* margarine, softened

1/2 cup granulated sugar

2 packages (3.52 ounces each) Swiss white
   confection with honey and almond
   nougat *or* 4 squares (4 ounces) white
   chocolate, chopped

1 cup toasted chopped almonds

1/4 cup chopped crystallized ginger

+ **HEAT** the oven to 325°F. Lightly butter and flour
   a large baking sheet.

+ **STIR** the eggs, instant coffee, and vanilla in a
   small bowl until well blended; set aside. Mix the
   flour, baking powder, and salt in a medium bowl;
   set aside.

+ **BEAT** the butter and sugar in a large bowl with an
   electric mixer set on medium speed until light and
   fluffy. Beat in the egg mixture. Gradually add the
   flour mixture, beating well after each addition. Stir
   in the white confection, almonds, and ginger.

+ **DIVIDE** the dough into two equal portions. On a
   lightly floured surface, shape the dough into 2
   logs, each 14 inches long, 1 1/2 inches wide, and 1
   inch thick. Place the logs 2 inches apart on the
   prepared baking sheet.

+ **BAKE** for 25 minutes or until lightly browned. Set
   the baking sheet on a wire rack for 10 minutes to
   cool. Remove the logs from the sheet and place on
   a cutting board. Using a serrated knife, cut each
   log diagonally into 3/4-inch-thick slices. Place the
   slices upright and 1/2 inch apart on the baking
   sheet. Bake for 10 minutes or until slightly dry.
   Remove the biscotti from the baking sheet. Cool
   completely on the wire rack. Store in a tightly
   covered container.

Makes about 3 dozen biscotti

cinnamon mocha
squares

Chocolate graham crackers form the easy crust for this frozen mocha-flavored pudding dessert.

Prep: 10 minutes • Freeze: 3 hours

15 whole chocolate graham crackers

2 packages (8 ounces each) cream cheese, softened

3½ cups cold milk

3 packages (4-serving size) chocolate flavor instant pudding and pie filling

1 tablespoon instant coffee

¼ teaspoon ground cinnamon

1 tub (8 ounces) frozen whipped topping, thawed, divided

1 square (1 ounce) semi-sweet chocolate, grated *or* 3 tablespoons chocolate sprinkles

◆ **LINE** a 13x9-inch pan with foil. Arrange half of the crackers to cover the bottom of the prepared pan, cutting them to fit, if necessary.

◆ **BEAT** the cream cheese in a large bowl with an electric mixer set on low speed until smooth. Gradually beat in 1 cup of the milk until well blended. Add the remaining milk, pudding mixes, instant coffee, and cinnamon. Beat for 2 minutes. (The mixture will be thick.) Gently stir in 2 cups of the whipped topping.

◆ **SPREAD** half of the pudding mixture over the crackers in the pan. Arrange the remaining crackers over the pudding in the pan. Top with the remaining pudding mixture. Spread the remaining whipped topping evenly over the pudding. Sprinkle with the grated chocolate.

◆ **FREEZE** for 3 hours or overnight. Cut into squares to serve. Garnish as desired. Store the leftover dessert in the freezer.

Makes 18 servings

COFFEE HOUSE TIP

In most cases, it is easier to neatly cut bar-shaped brownies, bars, and other desserts if you line the pan with foil first. For a 13x9-inch pan, line the pan so that the foil extends 2 inches beyond the two long sides of the pan. If indicated in the recipe, lightly butter the bottom and sides of the foil-lined pan. After baking (or in some cases, refrigerating or freezing), use the two ends of the foil as handles and lift the dessert out of the pan onto a cutting board. Cut into rectangles or squares. Use this same technique to line 8- and 9-inch square pans and loaf pans.

café au lait parfaits

This attractive layered pudding dessert looks especially inviting when served in clear dessert glasses or glass coffee mugs.

Prep: 15 minutes • Refrigerate: 2 hours

4 cups cold half-and-half *or* milk, divided

1 package (4-serving size) vanilla flavor instant pudding and pie filling

4 teaspoons instant coffee, divided

1 package (4-serving size) chocolate flavor instant pudding and pie filling

Whipped topping and cocoa powder *or* grated chocolate, for garnish (optional)

◆ **POUR** 2 cups of the cold half-and-half into a medium bowl. Add the vanilla flavor pudding mix and 2 teaspoons of the instant coffee. Beat with a wire whisk for 2 minutes or until well blended.

◆ **POUR** the remaining 2 cups of cold half-and-half into another medium bowl. Add the chocolate flavor pudding mix and the remaining 2 teaspoons of instant coffee. Beat with a wire whisk for 2 minutes or until well blended.

◆ **REMOVE** ²/₃ cup of each flavor of pudding from its bowl and whisk together in another medium bowl until well blended. Let all 3 pudding mixtures stand for 5 minutes.

◆ **SPOON** the chocolate pudding evenly into 6 dessert glasses. Layer with the chocolate-vanilla pudding mixture; then top with the vanilla pudding.

◆ **REFRIGERATE** for 2 hours or until ready to serve. Garnish with whipped topping and cocoa powder or grated chocolate, if desired.

Makes 6 servings

COFFEE HOUSE INSPIRATION

The topping on these parfaits is sprinkled with grated chocolate (see "Tips and Techniques" on page 20), but another garnish that would be delicious is toasted coconut. Toasting the coconut adds extra flavor. Spread the coconut in a shallow pan. Toast at 350°F for 7 to 12 minutes or until lightly browned, stirring frequently. Or, toast 1¹/₃ cups of coconut in a microwave oven on High for 5 minutes, stirring several times. Cool before sprinkling on desserts or beverages. Store in an tightly covered container in the freezer until ready to use.

café au lait parfait

fluffy coffee cheesecake

This light cheesecake makes any lunchtime affair seem more special.

Prep: 15 minutes • Refrigerate: 3 hours

2 tablespoons instant coffee

1 teaspoon vanilla extract

1 package (8 ounces) cream cheese, softened

1/3 cup granulated sugar

1 tub (8 ounces) frozen whipped topping, thawed

1 prepared graham cracker crust (6 ounces *or* 9 inches)

Raspberry sauce (recipe follows) for serving with pie (optional)

✦ **STIR** the instant coffee and vanilla in a small bowl until well blended; set aside.

✦ **BEAT** the cream cheese and sugar in a medium bowl with an electric mixer set on high speed until smooth. Stir in the coffee mixture. Gently stir in the whipped topping. Spoon the mixture into the crust.

✦ **REFRIGERATE** for 3 hours or until firm. Cut into slices to serve. Serve with the Raspberry Sauce, if desired. Store the leftover cheesecake in the refrigerator.

Makes 8 servings

raspberry sauce

Use this simple sauce to dress up your favorite desserts.

Prep: 5 minutes

1 package (10 ounces) frozen red raspberries in syrup, thawed

1/3 cup light corn syrup

✦ **PLACE** the raspberries in a blender container; cover. Blend until pureed. Strain to remove the seeds. Stir in the corn syrup.

✦ **REFRIGERATE** until ready to serve.

Makes about 1 1/3 cups sauce

coffee smoothie

Coffee and frozen yogurt combine to make this luscious smoothie.

Prep: 5 minutes

1 cup cold brewed coffee
1 cup coffee, vanilla *or* chocolate frozen yogurt
Additional frozen yogurt (optional)

◆ **PLACE** the coffee and frozen yogurt in a blender container; cover. Blend on high speed until smooth. Pour into tall glasses. Top each serving with scoops of additional frozen yogurt, if desired. Serve immediately.

Makes 2 servings

COFFEE HOUSE INSPIRATIONS

banana coffee smoothie: Add half of a small banana to the blender with the coffee and frozen yogurt.

chocolate coffee smoothie: Add 2 tablespoons of chocolate syrup to the blender with the coffee and frozen yogurt.

coffee soda

Instant coffee adds an extra "edge" to an ice-cold glass of cola.

Prep: 5 minutes

1 teaspoon instant coffee
2 tablespoons water
1 bottle (6 ½ ounces) cola beverage, chilled
Coffee Ice Cubes (page 97) *or* ice cubes
(optional)

◆ **PLACE** the instant coffee in a tall glass. Stir in the water until the coffee is completely dissolved. Add a small amount of the cola beverage. Stir in the remaining cola beverage. Add ice cubes, if desired. Serve immediately.

Makes 1 serving

COFFEE HOUSE INSPIRATION

Prepare the beverage as directed, substituting root beer or cream soda for the cola.

banana split cheesecake squares

A creamy coffee-banana cheesecake mixture crowns a buttery graham cracker crust, and is then topped with delectable fruit. For extra decadence, drizzle with melted chocolate and sprinkle with chopped nuts.

Prep: 20 minutes • Bake: 30 minutes • Refrigerate: 3 hours

CRUST:

2 cups graham cracker crumbs

⅓ cup butter *or* margarine, melted

¼ cup granulated sugar

FILLING:

3 large eggs

2 tablespoons instant coffee

3 packages (8 ounces each) cream cheese, softened

¾ cup granulated sugar

1 teaspoon vanilla extract

½ cup mashed ripe banana

TOPPING:

1 cup halved strawberries

1 banana, sliced, tossed with 1 teaspoon lemon juice

1 can (8 ounces) pineapple chunks, drained

Melted semi-sweet chocolate and chopped nuts (optional)

banana split cheesecake squares

PREPARE THE CRUST:

✦ **HEAT** the oven to 350°F. Line a 13x9-inch baking pan with foil.

✦ **MIX** the crumbs, butter, and sugar in a medium bowl. Press the mixture evenly onto the bottom of the prepared pan.

PREPARE THE FILLING:

✦ **STIR** the eggs and instant coffee in a small bowl until well blended; set aside.

✦ **BEAT** the cream cheese, sugar, and vanilla in a large bowl with an electric mixer set on medium speed until well blended. Add the egg mixture and mix until blended. Stir in the mashed banana. Spread the mixture evenly over the crust.

✦ **BAKE** for 30 minutes or until the center is almost set. Cool completely on a wire rack.

✦ **REFRIGERATE** for 3 hours or until ready to serve.

PREPARE THE TOPPING:

✦ **ARRANGE** the strawberries, sliced banana, and pineapple on top of the cheesecake. Drizzle with melted chocolate and sprinkle with nuts, if desired. Cut into squares to serve.

Makes 18 servings

sugar & spice coffee

Sugar and spice and everything nice—that's what this coffee beverage is made of!

Prep: 5 minutes

²/₃ cup ground coffee

1 teaspoon ground cinnamon

¼ cup granulated sugar *or* firmly
    packed brown sugar

6 cups cold water

Cinnamon sticks and orange peel strips
    (optional)

✦ **PLACE** the coffee and cinnamon in the filter in the brew basket of a coffee maker. Place the sugar in the empty pot of the coffee maker.

✦ **PREPARE** the coffee with the cold water. When the brewing is complete, stir until well mixed. Pour into large cups or mugs. Garnish with cinnamon sticks and orange peel strips, if desired.

Makes 6 servings.

COFFEE HOUSE INSPIRATION

For a Cool Variation: Prepare as directed and refrigerate for a cold beverage. Serve over ice.

orange cappuccino float

This creamy cappuccino shake served over orange sherbet is unbeatable.

Prep: 5 minutes

½ cup cold milk

1 envelope instant cappuccino mix, any flavor

1 pint vanilla ice cream (2 cups), softened
    Orange sherbet

✦ **PLACE** the cold milk and cappuccino mix in a

blender container; cover. Blend on high speed until the cappuccino mix is dissolved. Add the ice cream; cover. Blend until smooth. Pour over scoops of the sherbet in tall glasses. Serve immediately.

Makes 3 cups

thai coffee

Sweetened condensed milk is a popular ingredient in Thai food and beverage recipes. In this drink, it imparts a sweet, slightly caramel quality to the coffee.

Prep: 5 minutes

½ cup ground coffee
½ cup sweetened condensed milk
3 cups cold water

✦ **PLACE** the coffee in the filter in the brew basket of a coffee maker. Pour the condensed milk into the empty pot of the coffee maker.

✦ **PREPARE** the coffee with the cold water. When the brewing is complete, stir until well blended. Pour into large cups or mugs.

Makes 4 servings

COFFEE HOUSE INSPIRATION

For a Cool Variation: Prepare as directed and refrigerate for a cold beverage. Serve over ice.

mocha orange coffee

This trio of flavors harmonize beautifully.

Prep: 10 minutes

¾ cup ground coffee
1 tablespoon grated orange peel
⅓ cup chocolate syrup *or* dessert topping
4½ cups cold water
Whipped cream and ground cinnamon *or*
    ground nutmeg (optional)

✦ **PLACE** the coffee and orange peel in the filter in the brew basket of a coffee maker. Pour the chocolate syrup into the empty pot of the coffee maker.

✦ **PREPARE** the coffee with the cold water. When the brewing is complete, stir until well mixed. Pour into large cups or mugs. Top each serving with whipped cream and ground cinnamon or ground nutmeg, if desired. Serve immediately.

Makes 6 servings

café latte cheesecake

*This coffee-flavored cheesecake is delicious served with a dessert sauce
such as Easy Coffee Caramel Sauce (recipe follows).*

Prep. 15 minutes • Bake: 40 minutes • Refrigerate: 3 hours

2 packages (8 ounces each) cream cheese,
    softened

½ cup granulated sugar

2 large eggs

⅓ cup room-temperature brewed double-
    strength coffee

1 prepared graham cracker crumb crust
    (6 ounces *or* 9 inches)

Whipped cream, for piping on the pie (optional)

✦ **HEAT** the oven to 350°F.

✦ **BEAT** the cream cheese and sugar in a large bowl
with an electric mixer set on medium speed until
well blended. Add the eggs and coffee and mix
until blended. Pour the mixture into the crust.

✦ **BAKE** for 35 to 40 minutes or until the center is
almost set. Cool completely on a wire rack.

✦ **REFRIGERATE** for at least 3 hours or overnight.
Cut into slices to serve. Using a pastry bag fitted
with a star tip, pipe the whipped cream, if desired.
Store the leftover cheesecake in the refrigerator.

Makes 8 servings

easy coffee caramel sauce

This is also a superb sauce for ice cream and other desserts.

Prep: 10 minutes

1 cup caramel dessert topping

2 tablespoons brewed strong coffee

✦ **HEAT** the dessert topping and coffee in a small
saucepan on low heat, stirring constantly, until

well mixed and warm. Serve warm. Store the
leftover sauce in the refrigerator. Reheat before
serving.

Makes about 1 cup

*café latte cheesecake with
easy coffee caramel sauce*

easy mocha cookies

Next time you want milk and cookies, think of these fast-to-make treats.

Prep: 10 minutes • Bake: 9 minutes

4 squares (4 ounces) unsweetened chocolate
½ cup (1 stick) butter *or* margarine, softened
1¼ cups granulated sugar
1 large egg
1 teaspoon vanilla extract
⅓ cup milk
1¼ cups all-purpose flour
2 tablespoons instant coffee
2 teaspoons baking powder

+ **HEAT** the oven to 350°F.

+ **MICROWAVE** the chocolate in a large microwavable bowl on High for 1½ minutes or until the chocolate is almost melted, stirring halfway through the cooking time. Stir until the chocolate is completely melted.

+ **BEAT** in the butter and sugar with an electric mixer set on medium speed until well blended. Beat in the egg and vanilla. Mix in the milk. On low speed, stir in the flour, instant coffee, and baking powder. Drop by tablespoonfuls, 2 inches apart, onto ungreased baking sheets.

+ **BAKE** for 9 minutes or until the cookies are puffed and a slight indentation remains when touched lightly. Set the baking sheets on wire racks to cool for 1 minute. Using a metal spatula, transfer the cookies to the wire racks. Cool completely. Store in a tightly covered container.

Makes about 3 dozen cookies

coffee milk

An ordinary glass of milk becomes extraordinary when you stir in instant coffee.

Prep: 5 minutes

1 teaspoon instant coffee

1 cup cold milk

Ice cubes (optional)

COFFEE HOUSE INSPIRATION

Stir in chocolate syrup or malted milk powder to taste.

✦ **PLACE** the instant coffee in a tall glass. Add a small amount of milk and stir until the coffee is dissolved. Stir in the remaining milk. Serve with ice cubes, and sweeten to taste, if desired.

Makes 1 serving

coffee ice cubes

These ice cubes are great with any iced coffee drink.

Prep: 5 minutes

✦ **POUR** cooled brewed coffee into ice cube trays. Freeze until solid.

✦ **USE** to chill coffee beverages without diluting the flavor.

COFFEE HOUSE INSPIRATION

For a mocha experience, use these coffee ice cubes in a beverage that is half cold brewed coffee and half cold chocolate milk.

afternoon coffee time

By mid-afternoon, your energy may be flagging
a little. No wonder the British have long known that
tea time is the only civilized way to get re-energized.
Following in their footsteps, Americans are always ready
with a fork held high to greet *coffee napoleons
with strawberries* (page 102) or a
sweet *berry mocha tart* (page 107).
In this chapter, you'll also find some fabulous recipes for
cookies, scones, and muffins to enjoy with a
cup of hot or iced coffee.

coffee macadamia nut pie
coffee cinnamon cookies
coffee napoleons with strawberries
coffee shortbread sticks
granita de caffe
berry mocha tart
cappuccino white chocolate chunk muffins
coffee jelly roll
coffee lace cookies
nutty coffee bars
coffee raisin scones
caffe panna cotta
chocolate nut biscotti
mocha cherry almond biscotti
cappuccino swirl cheesecake
hot white chocolate coffee
fruity coffee
shake sensation
spiced brazilian chocolate
two-toned biscotti
chocolate almond coffee
easy iced coffee latte
hot cappuccino float
old-fashioned coffee sodas

coffee macadamia
nut pie

Accented with coffee and chock full of coconut and macadamia nuts,
this flavorful pie will take you on a taste trip to Hawaii.

Prep: 15 minutes • Bake: 60 minutes

¼ cup heavy (whipping) cream

1 tablespoon instant coffee

3 large eggs, lightly beaten

1 cup light corn syrup

1 cup granulated sugar

1 tablespoon butter *or* margarine, melted

1 cup sweetened flaked coconut

1 jar (3 ½ ounces) macadamia nuts, coarsely chopped (about ¾ cup)

1 unbaked pie crust (9-inch)

✦ **HEAT** the oven to 350°F.

✦ **STIR** the cream and instant coffee in a large bowl until well blended. Stir in the eggs, corn syrup, sugar, and butter. Stir in the coconut and nuts. Pour the mixture into the crust.

✦ **BAKE** for 50 to 60 minutes or until a knife inserted halfway between the center and the edge comes out clean. Cool completely on a wire rack. Cut into slices to serve.

Makes 8 servings

COFFEE HOUSE TIP

Substitute ¾ cup coarsely chopped almonds, pecans, or walnuts for the macadamia nuts.

A DROP OF HISTORY

1892   Joel Cheek perfects his efforts at blending several top-quality types of coffee beans into a new, superior flavor and convinces the management of the Maxwell House Hotel to serve the coffee exclusively to their guests. This special blend soon becomes known as Maxwell House coffee.

coffee cinnamon cookies

These tender shortbread-type cookies are perfect for dunking in a cup of coffee. Or scoop Coffee Ice Cream (page 195) into stemmed dessert glasses and serve with a plate of these cookies.

Prep: 15 minutes • Bake: 25 minutes

1 tablespoon instant coffee

1 teaspoon vanilla extract

1 cup all-purpose flour

½ cup cornstarch

½ cup powdered sugar

¼ teaspoon ground cinnamon

1 cup butter *or* margarine, softened

◆ **HEAT** the oven to 300°F.

◆ **STIR** the instant coffee and vanilla in a small bowl until well blended; set aside. Mix the flour, cornstarch, sugar, and cinnamon in a small bowl; set aside.

◆ **BEAT** the butter in a large bowl with an electric mixer set on medium speed. Add the coffee and flour mixtures and beat until well blended. If necessary, cover and refrigerate until the dough is firm enough to handle. Shape into 1-inch balls. Place the balls 1½ inches apart on ungreased baking sheets. Flatten each ball with a lightly floured fork.

◆ **BAKE** for 20 to 25 minutes or until the edges are lightly browned. Set the baking sheets on wire racks to cool for 5 minutes. Using a metal spatula, transfer the cookies to the wire racks. Cool completely. Store in a tightly covered container.

Makes about 2 dozen cookies

COFFEE HOUSE INSPIRATION

Use a fork dipped in powdered sugar instead of the flour to flatten the balls of cookie dough.

coffee napoleons
with strawberries

Flaky puff pastry is layered with a rich coffee and white chocolate filling and colorful sliced strawberries.

Prep: 20 minutes • Bake: 15 minutes

½ package (17 ¼ ounces) frozen puff pastry sheets, thawed

1 cup cold half-and-half

1 tablespoon instant coffee

1 package white chocolate *or* vanilla flavor instant pudding and pie filling

1 tub (8 ounces) frozen whipped topping, thawed

2 pints strawberries, sliced

Powdered sugar for sprinkling on the napoleons

Fresh mint sprigs, for garnish (optional)

✦ **HEAT** the oven to 400°F.

✦ **UNFOLD** the pastry on a lightly floured surface. Cut into 3 strips along the fold marks. Cut each strip into 4 rectangles. Place 2 inches apart on a baking sheet.

✦ **BAKE** for 15 minutes or until golden. Remove the pastries from the baking sheet. Cool completely on a wire rack.

✦ **STIR** the cold half-and-half and instant coffee in a large bowl until well blended. Add the pudding mix. Beat with a wire whisk for 1 minute. Let stand for 5 minutes. Gently stir in the whipped topping.

✦ **CUT** each pastry into 2 layers, making 24 layers in all. Set aside 8 top layers. Spread 8 bottom layers with 2 tablespoons of the pudding mixture and sliced strawberries. Repeat the layers, and top with the reserved top layers. Sprinkle with powdered sugar. Garnish with the mint sprigs, if desired. Serve immediately or refrigerate for up to 4 hours.

Makes 8 napoleons

COFFEE HOUSE INSPIRATIONS

For the simplest of desserts, just spoon this coffee filling into stemmed glasses alternately with the sliced strawberries. It would also be delicious served in baked puff pastry shells or individual graham cracker crusts.

coffee napoleon with strawberries

coffee shortbread
sticks

These buttery shortbreads are flavored with coffee and a hint of cinnamon.

Prep: 10 minutes • Bake: 35 minutes

2 tablespoons instant coffee

1 teaspoon vanilla extract

3 cups all-purpose flour

1 teaspoon salt

$\frac{1}{4}$ teaspoon ground cinnamon

1$\frac{1}{4}$ cups (2$\frac{1}{2}$ sticks) butter, softened

1$\frac{1}{4}$ cups powdered sugar

Additional powdered sugar for sprinkling on the shortbread sticks (optional)

✦ **HEAT** the oven to 325°F.

✦ **STIR** the instant coffee and vanilla in a small bowl until well blended; set aside. Mix the flour, salt, and cinnamon in a medium bowl; set aside.

✦ **BEAT** the butter in a large bowl with an electric mixer set on medium speed until smooth and creamy. Gradually add the 1$\frac{1}{4}$ cups powdered sugar, beating until well blended. Beat in the coffee mixture. Add the flour mixture and beat on low speed until blended. Press the mixture firmly into the bottom of a 13x9-inch baking pan. Pierce the entire dough at 1-inch intervals with a fork.

✦ **BAKE** for 30 to 35 minutes or until the edges are lightly browned. Set the pan on a wire rack to cool for 5 minutes. Cut the shortbread into bars while warm. Cool completely on the wire rack. Sprinkle with the additional powdered sugar, if desired. Store in a tightly covered container.

Makes about 2 dozen cookies

granita di caffe

On a hot afternoon, this icy coffee dessert will cool you right down.

Prep: 5 minutes • Freeze: 4½ hours

2 cups hot freshly brewed strong coffee

½ cup granulated sugar

2 teaspoons vanilla extract

Whipped cream and chocolate curls, for
  garnish (optional)

✦ **STIR** the hot coffee and the sugar in a medium
  bowl until the sugar is dissolved. Mix in the
  vanilla. Pour the mixture into an 8-inch-square
  pan.

✦ **FREEZE** for about 1½ hours or until almost firm.
  Using a fork, break up into small pieces. Freeze for
  about 3 hours longer or until firm. Break up into
  small pieces again with a fork. Spoon into chilled
  dessert glasses. Garnish with whipped cream and
  chocolate curls, if desired.

Makes 4 servings

COFFEE HOUSE INSPIRATIONS

granita di caffe latte: Prepare as directed,
increasing the sugar to ¾ cup. Stir 1 cup
of milk into the coffee mixture before
freezing.

mochaccino granita di caffe: Prepare as
directed, decreasing the sugar to ¼ cup.
Stir ⅔ cup vanilla ice cream, softened, and
2 tablespoons of chocolate syrup into the
coffee mixture before freezing. To double
the chocolate flavor, substitute chocolate
ice cream for the vanilla ice cream.

berry mocha tart

A buttery almond crust is filled with ganache—a decadent mixture of chocolate and cream. Our variation is particularly intense because of the addition of coffee. An artful arrangement of fresh berries is its crowning glory.

Prep: 25 minutes • Bake: 10 minutes

TOASTED ALMOND TART SHELL:

1 cup all-purpose flour

¼ cup granulated sugar

⅓ cup butter *or* margarine

½ cup finely chopped toasted almonds
   (see Coffee House Tips)

2 tablespoons cold water

MOCHA GANACHE:

⅓ cup heavy (whipping) cream

2 tablespoons instant coffee

4 squares (4 ounces) semi-sweet chocolate,
   cut into chunks

1 pint strawberries, sliced *or* ½ pint raspberries

Fresh mint sprig, for garnish (optional)

**PREPARE THE TOASTED ALMOND
TART SHELL:**

✦ **HEAT** the oven to 350°F.

✦ **MIX** the flour and sugar in a medium bowl. Using a pastry blender or 2 knives, cut in the butter until the mixture resembles coarse crumbs. Stir in the almonds. Add the water and stir until the mixture forms a ball. Press the dough onto the bottom and up the sides of a 9-inch tart pan.

✦ **BAKE** for 10 minutes or until lightly browned. Cool completely on a wire rack.

PREPARE THE MOCHA GANACHE:

✦ **STIR** the cream and instant coffee in a medium microwavable bowl until well blended. Add the chocolate.

✦ **MICROWAVE** on High for 2 minutes, stirring halfway through cooking time. Stir until the chocolate is completely melted. As the mixture cools, it will thicken. Spread the ganache in the tart shell. Arrange the berries on top.

✦ **REFRIGERATE** until ready to serve. Cut into slices to serve.

Makes 8 servings

COFFEE HOUSE TIPS

Toast the nuts BEFORE finely chopping them. Spread the nuts in a shallow pan. Toast at 400°F for 8 to 10 minutes or until golden, stirring frequently.

For a quick crust, line the 9-inch tart pan with a ready-made refrigerated crust and bake according to the package directions.

berry mocha tart

cappuccino white chocolate chunk muffins

Chunks of white chocolate work deliciously in these cappuccino-flavored muffins.

Prep: 15 minutes • Bake: 20 minutes

2 cups all-purpose flour

½ cup granulated sugar

2 envelopes instant cappuccino mix, any flavor

2½ teaspoons baking powder

½ teaspoon ground cinnamon

½ teaspoon salt

1 large egg

1 cup milk

½ cup (1 stick) butter *or* margarine, melted

4 squares (4 ounces) white chocolate, chopped

✦ **HEAT** the oven to 375°F. Lightly butter 12 muffin pan cups (or line them with paper cups).

✦ **STIR** the flour, sugar, cappuccino mixes, baking powder, cinnamon, and salt in a large bowl. Beat the egg in a medium bowl. Stir in the milk and butter. Add the egg mixture to the flour mixture and stir just until moistened. Stir in the chocolate. Spoon the batter into the prepared muffin cups, filling each cup two-thirds full.

✦ **BAKE** for 15 to 20 minutes or until a toothpick inserted in the center of one muffin comes out clean. Remove the pan to a wire rack and cool for 5 minutes. Remove the muffins from the pan and cool on the wire rack. Serve warm.

Makes 1 dozen muffins

coffee jelly roll

Fill this traditional cake with your favorite jam or jelly.

Prep: 15 minutes • Bake:15 minutes

1 cup all-purpose flour

1 teaspoon baking powder

5 tablespoons hot water

2 tablespoons butter *or* margarine

1 tablespoon instant coffee

3 large eggs, at room temperature

1 teaspoon vanilla extract

1/4 teaspoon salt

1 cup granulated sugar

Powdered sugar for sprinkling on the
cloth towel and over the jelly roll

1 cup apricot jam *or* jelly

✦ **HEAT** the oven to 375°F. Butter a 15x10-inch baking pan. Line with wax paper; butter the wax paper.

✦ **MIX** the flour and baking powder in a small bowl; set aside. Heat the water, butter, and instant coffee in a small saucepan on medium heat until the butter is melted; set aside.

✦ **BEAT** the eggs, vanilla, and salt in a large bowl with an electric mixer set on high speed. Gradually add the granulated sugar, beating until thick and light in color. Gently stir in the flour mixture. Add the butter mixture; gently stir until well blended. Spread the batter in the prepared pan.

✦ **BAKE** for 12 to 15 minutes or until a toothpick inserted in the center of the cake comes out clean. Generously sprinkle a cloth towel with the powdered sugar. Turn the cake out onto the towel. Carefully remove the wax paper. Trim any crisp edges, if necessary. Roll the cake up in the towel, starting with the short side. Cool completely on a wire rack. Unroll the cake. Spread with the jam; reroll the cake. Before serving, sprinkle the cake with additional powdered sugar, if desired. Cut into slices to serve.

Makes 8 servings

ENTERTAINING IDEA

Instead of an afternoon tea party, why not have a coffee party? Get out your best dishes and serve any of the recipes from this cookbook. Of course, the recipes in this chapter are a natural. For a "hot, lazy summer afternoon" variation on this theme, serve cold coffee beverages. Make sure to check out "Serving Coffee with Style" (page 16).

coffee lace
cookies

*These delicate cookies can be rolled around a wooden spoon handle or left flat,
as you prefer. If you like, you can stripe them with melted dark or white chocolate.*

Prep: 15 minutes • Bake: 7 minutes

¼ cup granulated sugar

¼ cup butter *or* margarine

¼ cup light corn syrup

½ cup all-purpose flour

¼ cup finely chopped almonds, pecans,
    or walnuts

2 tablespoons instant coffee

✦ **HEAT** the oven to 350°F. Cover 2 baking sheets
with aluminum foil with the dull side up. Spray
with no-stick cooking spray.

✦ **MIX** the sugar, butter, and corn syrup in a small
saucepan. Stirring constantly, bring the mixture to
a boil over medium heat. Remove the pan from
the heat. Stir in the flour, nuts, and instant coffee.
Drop 6 to 8 evenly spaced scant teaspoonfuls of
batter onto each of the prepared baking sheets.

✦ **BAKE** for 7 minutes or until the cookies are gold-
en.Set the baking sheets on wire racks to cool for
1 to 2 minutes or until the cookies can be lifted
but are still warm and soft. Carefully remove them
with a metal spatula and roll each cookie around
the handle of a wooden spoon. Slide off the
cookies when they are set. (If the cookies harden
before they can be rolled, return them to the oven
for 30 seconds to soften.) Cool the cookies
completely on the wire racks. Store in a tightly
covered container.

Makes about 2 ½ dozen cookies.

COFFEE HOUSE INSPIRATION

**For an easy Napoleon-style dessert, do not
roll the cookies after baking. Set them flat
on a wire rack to cool completely. Layer
the cookies with small scoops of softened
ice cream. Serve with your favorite dessert
sauce.**

coffee lace cookies with nutty coffee bars (page 112)
and coffee raisin scones (page 113)

nutty coffee bars

In these bars, a buttery shortbread crust is topped with a very nutty mixture.
The rich result is somewhat reminiscent of pecan pie.

Prep: 15 minutes • Bake: 45 minutes

SHORTBREAD CRUST:

1¼ cups all-purpose flour

¼ cup granulated sugar

½ cup (1 stick) butter *or* margarine

NUTTY TOPPING:

1 large egg

1 tablespoon instant coffee

½ cup firmly packed brown sugar

⅓ cup corn syrup

2 tablespoons butter *or* margarine, melted

1 teaspoon vanilla extract

1½ cups chopped walnuts, pecans *or* almonds

PREPARE THE SHORTBREAD CRUST:

✦ **HEAT** the oven to 375⁰F. Line a 9-inch square baking pan with foil; lightly butter the foil.

✦ **MIX** the flour and granulated sugar in a medium bowl. Using a pastry blender or 2 knives, cut in the butter until the mixture resembles coarse crumbs. Press the mixture firmly into the bottom of the prepared pan.

✦ **BAKE** for 15 to 20 minutes or until very lightly browned. Remove the pan from the oven to a wire rack. Cool slightly.

PREPARE THE NUTTY TOPPING:

✦ **STIR** the egg and instant coffee in a medium bowl until well blended. Stir in the brown sugar, corn syrup, butter, and vanilla until well blended. Stir in the nuts. Spread the mixture evenly over the warm crust.

✦ **BAKE** for 20 to 25 minutes or until the topping is firm around the edges and slightly soft in the center. Cool the bars completely on a wire rack. Cut into bars to serve. Store in a tightly covered container.

Makes 18 bars

COFFEE HOUSE TIP

This recipe can be doubled. Press the crust mixture firmly onto the bottom of a buttered foil-lined 15x10x1-inch baking pan. Bake for 20 minutes or until very lightly browned. Spread the topping over the warm crust. Bake for 15 to 20 minutes or until the topping is firm around the edges and slightly soft in the center.

Makes 3 dozen bars

coffee raisin
scones

Serve these tender scones warm or cool them slightly
and decorate with a coffee-flavored glaze.

Prep: 20 minutes • Bake: 12 minutes

1¾ cups all-purpose flour
2 tablespoons granulated sugar
2½ teaspoons baking powder
½ teaspoon salt
6 tablespoons butter *or* margarine
2 large eggs
¼ cup milk
1 tablespoon instant coffee
½ cup raisins

✦ **HEAT** the oven to 425°F. Lightly butter a large baking sheet.

✦ **MIX** the flour, granulated sugar, baking powder, and salt in a large bowl. Using a pastry blender or 2 knives, cut in the butter until the mixture resembles coarse crumbs. Beat the eggs in a small bowl; stir in the milk and instant coffee. Add to the flour mixture. Stir until a soft dough forms. Stir in the raisins.

✦ **KNEAD** the dough on a lightly floured surface until smooth. Pat into a 12x4-inch rectangle. With a sharp knife, cut the dough into 4-inch squares. Cut each square into 4 triangles. Place the scones on the prepared baking sheet.

✦ **BAKE** for 10 to 12 minutes or until golden brown. Remove the scones from the baking sheet and cool slightly on a wire rack. Serve warm. If desired, glaze the scones with Easy Coffee Glaze (see below).

Makes 1 dozen scones

COFFEE HOUSE INSPIRATION

Easy Coffee Glaze: Stir 1 tablespoon of water and ¼ teaspoon of instant coffee in a small bowl until well blended. Add ½ cup of powdered sugar and mix well. Drizzle the glaze over the warm scones.

caffe panna cotta

Coffee adds depth to these traditional Italian custard desserts.
Place each dessert in the center of a larger plate and make it look
spectacular with criss-crosses of chocolate and the sparkle of fresh oranges..

Prep: 10 minutes • Cook: 15 minutes • Refrigerate: 4 hours

2 cups milk

2 tablespoons instant coffee

2 envelopes unflavored gelatin

2 cups heavy (whipping) cream

1¼ cups powdered sugar

1 teaspoon vanilla extract

⅛ teaspoon ground cinnamon

Orange slices and melted semi-sweet and
white chocolates, for garnish (optional)

◆ **BUTTER** eight 6-ounce ramekins or custard cups
lightly.

◆ **STIR** the milk and instant coffee in a medium
bowl until well blended. Remove ¼ cup of the
milk mixture to a small bowl. Sprinkle the gelatin
over the milk mixture and stir until blended. Set
aside until the milk is absorbed and the gelatin is
softened.

◆ **MIX** the remaining milk mixture, sugar, and
cream in a large saucepan. Whisking constantly,
bring the mixture just to a boil over medium heat.
Remove the pan from the heat. Add the softened
gelatin mixture, vanilla, and cinnamon. Whisk
until the gelatin is completely dissolved. Divide
the mixture evenly among the prepared ramekins.

◆ **REFRIGERATE** for 4 hours or until set. To serve,
run a sharp knife along the inside of each
ramekin. Invert the dessert onto a plate, shaking
to loosen the dessert. Garnish with orange slices
and melted semi-sweet and white chocolates, if
desired. Store leftover desserts in the refrigerator.

Makes 8 servings

COFFEE HOUSE INSPIRATION

**Drizzling desserts or dessert plates with
thin lines of melted chocolate can help you
present your desserts like a pro. See our
easy technique on page 20.**

caffe panna cotta

chocolate nut biscotti

Swiss bittersweet chocolate with honey and almond nougat is a wonderful addition to these crisp biscotti. Dipping them into melted chocolate makes them ultimately decadent.

Prep: 20 minutes • Bake: 35 minutes

2 large eggs

2 tablespoons instant coffee

1 teaspoon vanilla extract

2 cups all-purpose flour

1½ teaspoons baking powder

¼ teaspoon salt

½ cup (1 stick) butter *or* margarine, softened

¾ cup granulated sugar

1 cup chopped nuts

4 ounces Swiss bittersweet chocolate with honey and almond nougat, chopped

✦ **HEAT** the oven to 325°F. Lightly butter and flour a large baking sheet.

✦ **STIR** the eggs, instant coffee, and vanilla in a small bowl until well blended; set aside. Mix the flour, baking powder, and salt in a medium bowl; set aside.

✦ **BEAT** the butter and sugar in a large bowl with an electric mixer set on medium speed until light and fluffy. Beat in the egg mixture. Gradually add the flour mixture, beating well after each addition. Stir in the nuts and chocolate.

✦ **DIVIDE** the dough into 2 equal portions. On a lightly floured surface, shape the dough into

2 logs, each 14 inches long, 1½ inches wide, and 1 inch thick. Place the logs 2 inches apart on the prepared baking sheet.

✦ **BAKE** for 25 minutes or until lightly browned. Set the baking sheet on a wire rack to cool for 10 minutes. Remove the logs from the baking sheet and place on a cutting board. Using a serrated knife, cut each log diagonally into ¾-inch-thick slices. Place the slices upright and ½ inch apart on the baking sheet. Bake for 10 minutes or until slightly dry. Remove the biscotti from the baking sheet. Cool completely on the wire rack. Store in a tightly covered container.

Makes about 3 dozen biscotti

COFFEE HOUSE INSPIRATIONS

For chocolate-dipped biscotti, melt 8 squares (8 ounces) of semi-sweet chocolate. Dip each of the biscotti halfway into the melted chocolate. Let the excess chocolate drip off. Place the biscotti on a wax paper-lined tray. Refrigerate until the chocolate is firm.

Bittersweet *or* semi-sweet chocolate can be substituted for the Swiss chocolate. Use 4 squares (4 ounces).

mocha cherry
almond biscotti

Cherries and toasted almonds partner beautifully in these mocha-flavored biscotti.

Prep: 20 minutes • Bake: 35 minutes

2 large eggs

2 tablespoons instant coffee

1 teaspoon vanilla extract

2 ½ cups all-purpose flour

1 ½ teaspoons baking powder

¼ teaspoon salt

½ cup (1 stick) **butter** *or* **margarine softened**

¾ cup granulated sugar

1 square (1 ounce) semi-sweet chocolate, melted, cooled

1 cup chopped toasted almonds

½ cup dried cherries

✦ **HEAT** the oven to 325°F. Lightly butter and flour a large baking sheet.

✦ **STIR** the eggs, instant coffee, and vanilla in a small bowl until well blended; set aside. Mix the flour, baking powder, and salt in a small bowl; set aside.

✦ **BEAT** the butter and sugar in a large bowl with an electric mixer set on medium speed until light and fluffy. Beat in the egg mixture. Gradually add the flour mixture, beating well after each addition. Stir in the chocolate until well blended. Stir in the almonds and cherries.

✦ **DIVIDE** the dough into 2 equal portions. On a lightly floured surface, shape the dough into 2 logs, each 14 inches long, 1 ½ inches wide, and 1 inch thick. Place the logs 2 inches apart on the prepared baking sheet.

✦ **BAKE** for 25 minutes or until lightly browned. Set the baking sheet on a wire rack to cool for 10 minutes. Remove the logs from the baking sheet and place on a cutting board. Using a serrated knife, cut each log diagonally into ¾-inch-thick slices. Place the slices upright and ½-inch apart on the baking sheet. Bake for 10 minutes or until slightly dry. Remove the biscotti from the baking sheet. Cool completely on the wire rack. Store in a tightly covered container.

Makes about 3 dozen biscotti

COFFEE HOUSE INSPIRATION

Toast the almonds *before* chopping to add extra flavor. To toast nuts, spread them in a shallow pan. Toast at 400°F for 8 to 10 minutes or until the nuts are golden, stirring frequently.

cappuccino swirl cheesecake

In this easy and appealing cheesecake, a chocolate crumb crust is filled with a coffee-flavored cream cheese batter, then topped with swirls of a cinnamon batter.

Prep: 15 minutes • Bake: 35 minutes • Refrigerate: 3 hours

2 packages (8 ounces each) cream cheese, softened

½ cup granulated sugar

½ teaspoon vanilla extract

2 large eggs

⅛ teaspoon ground cinnamon

2 tablespoons instant coffee

1 prepared chocolate flavor crumb crust (6 ounces *or* 9 inches)

Chocolate sauce for drizzling on dessert plates (optional)

✦ **HEAT** the oven to 350°F.

✦ **BEAT** the cream cheese, sugar, and vanilla in a large bowl with an electric mixer set on medium speed until well blended. Add the eggs and mix until blended. Stir the cinnamon into 1 cup of the batter in a small bowl. Stir the instant coffee into the remaining batter. Pour the coffee mixture into the crust. Spoon the cinnamon batter over the coffee batter. Swirl with a knife to marbleize.

✦ **BAKE** for 35 minutes or until the center is almost set. Cool completely on a wire rack.

✦ **REFRIGERATE** for at least 3 hours or overnight. Cut into slices. Drizzle each plate with chocolate sauce, if desired. Store the leftover cheesecake in the refrigerator.

Makes 8 servings

COFFEE HOUSE TIP

You can soften cream cheese quickly in the microwave. Place 1 completely unwrapped package of cream cheese in a microwavable bowl. Microwave on High for 15 seconds. Add 15 seconds for each additional package of cream cheese.

cappuccino swirl cheesecake

hot white chocolate coffee

White chocolate and coffee join together to create this warming beverage.

Prep: 5 minutes

3 squares (3 ounces) white chocolate, chopped
2 cups half-and-half *or* whole milk
2 cups hot freshly brewed coffee
Whipped cream and chocolate curls (optional)

✦ **MICROWAVE** the chocolate and half-and-half in a medium microwavable bowl on HIGH for 2 minutes, stirring halfway through cooking time. Stir until the chocolate is completely melted and the mixture is smooth.

✦ **STIR** in the coffee. Pour into large cups or mugs. Top each serving with whipped cream and chocolate curls, if desired. Serve immediately.

Makes 6 servings

fruity coffee

Serve this beverage after a day of viewing fall foliage or selecting just the right pumpkin.

Prep: 10 minutes

3 cups hot freshly brewed coffee
¼ cup firmly packed brown sugar
4 whole cloves
½ cup orange juice

✦ **STIR** the hot coffee, sugar, and cloves in a heatproof container until the sugar is dissolved. Let stand for 5 minutes. Strain out the cloves. Stir in the orange juice. Serve warm without milk.

Makes 5 servings

COFFEE HOUSE INSPIRATION

For a variation using instant coffee, place ¼ cup of instant coffee, the brown sugar, and the cloves in a heatproof container or carafe. Add 3 cups of boiling water and stir until the sugar is dissolved. Continue as directed.

shake sensation

Looking for a delicious way to rejuvenate? This shake could be just the solution.

Prep: 5 minutes

½ cup cold brewed double-strength coffee

1 pint coffee, chocolate, *or* vanilla ice cream (2 cups), softened

✦ **PLACE** the coffee and ice cream in a blender container; cover. Blend on high speed using an on/off action until smooth. Pour into tall glasses. Serve immediately.

Makes 2 servings

spiced brazilian chocolate

If you would rather be in Rio, give this Brazilian-style coffee a try.

Prep: 10 minutes • Cook: 10 minutes

2 cups hot freshly brewed coffee

1 square (1 ounce) unsweetened chocolate, chopped

¼ cup granulated sugar

1 teaspoon ground cinnamon

1½ cups milk

1½ teaspoons vanilla extract

Whipped cream, orange peel, and/or additional ground cinnamon (optional)

✦ **HEAT** the coffee and chocolate in a heavy saucepan on very low heat until the chocolate is melted and the mixture is smooth, stirring constantly with a wire whisk.

✦ **STIR** in the sugar and cinnamon. Bring to a boil. Stir until the sugar is dissolved. Gradually stir in the milk and vanilla. Stirring occasionally, heat thoroughly. Pour into large cups or mugs. Top each serving with whipped cream and orange peel or additional ground cinnamon, if desired. Serve immediately.

Makes 7 servings

two-toned biscotti

These biscotti combine chocolate and coffee doughs to produce one crisp cookie. Perfect for a mid-afternoon breather.

Prep: 25 minutes • Bake: 40 minutes

2 large eggs

2 tablespoons instant coffee

1 teaspoon vanilla extract

2½ cups all-purpose flour

1½ teaspoons baking powder

¼ teaspoon salt

½ cup (1 stick) butter *or* margarine, softened

¾ cup granulated sugar

1 square (1 ounce) semi-sweet chocolate, melted, cooled

1 cup toasted chopped pecans

+ **HEAT** the oven to 325°F. Lightly butter and flour a large baking sheet.

+ **STIR** the eggs, instant coffee, and vanilla in a small bowl until well blended; set aside. Mix the flour, baking powder, and salt in a small bowl; set aside.

+ **BEAT** the butter and sugar in a large bowl with an electric mixer set on medium speed until light and fluffy. Beat in the egg mixture. Gradually add the flour mixture, beating well after each addition. Stir in the pecans. Remove half of the dough from the bowl; set aside. Add the melted chocolate to the dough remaining in the bowl and beat on low speed for about 1 minute or until well mixed.

+ **DIVIDE** both the chocolate and coffee doughs into 2 equal portions. On a lightly floured surface, shape each portion into a 6-inch-long log. Place one chocolate roll and one coffee roll side by side. Shape into a log 10 inches long, 1½ inches wide, and 1 inch thick. Repeat to form a second log. Place the logs 2 inches apart on the prepared baking sheet.

+ **BAKE** for 30 minutes or until lightly browned. Set the baking sheet on a wire rack for 10 minutes to cool. Remove the logs from the baking sheet and place on a cutting board. Using a serrated knife, cut each log diagonally into ½-inch-thick slices. Place the slices upright and ½ inch apart on the baking sheet. Bake for 10 minutes or until slightly dry. Remove the biscotti from the baking sheet. Cool completely on the wire rack. Store in a tightly covered container.

Makes about 2½ dozen biscotti

two-toned biscotti with hot white chocolate coffee (page 120)

chocolate almond coffee

Serve this coffee to satisfy a sweet tooth and a chocolate craving simultaneously.

Prep: 10 minutes

¼ cup ground coffee

2 tablespoons granulated sugar

2½ cups cold water

¼ teaspoon almond extract

1 cup half-and-half *or* whole milk

2 squares (2 ounces) semi-sweet chocolate, chopped

Whipped cream and chocolate curls (optional)

✦ **PLACE** the coffee in the filter in the brew basket of a coffee maker. Place the sugar in the empty pot of the coffee maker.

✦ **PREPARE** the coffee with the cold water. When the brewing is complete, stir in the almond extract until well mixed.

✦ **MICROWAVE** the half-and-half and chocolate in a medium microwavable bowl on High for 1 minute. Stir until the chocolate is completely melted and the mixture is smooth. Stir into the brewed flavored coffee. Pour into large cups or mugs. Top each serving with whipped cream and chocolate curls, if desired. Serve immediately.

Makes 6 servings

easy iced coffee latte

If you are looking to take a break on the porch, here's a refreshing beverage that you can stir together in a hurry. It fills a pitcher generously, so once it's made, you can relax.

Prep: 5 minutes

¼ cup instant coffee

¼ cup hot water

4 cups cold milk

Ice cubes

✦ **PLACE** the instant coffee in a large pitcher. Stir in the water until the instant coffee is dissolved. Stir in the milk. Sweeten to taste, if desired. Pour into ice-filled glasses.

Makes 6 servings

hot cappuccino float

This variation on a float uses hot cappuccino instead of soda.

Prep: 5 minutes

¼ cup coffee, chocolate, *or* vanilla ice cream

1 envelope instant cappuccino mix, any flavor

1 cup hot milk

♦ **PLACE** the ice cream in a large cup or mug. Prepare the cappuccino mix as directed on the package substituting the 1 cup of hot milk for the hot water. Pour over the ice cream. Serve immediately.

Makes 1 serving

old-fashioned
coffee sodas

Serve these fizzy sodas with a long spoon and a straw.

Prep: 5 minutes

3 cups cold brewed double-strength coffee

1 cup half-and-half *or* whole milk

2 tablespoons granulated sugar

Coffee ice cream

Chilled club soda

♦ **MIX** the coffee, half-and-half, and sugar in a large pitcher. Refrigerate until ready to serve. Place scoops of ice cream in tall glasses. Add ½ cup of the coffee mixture to each glass. Fill the glasses to the top with the soda. Serve immediately.

Makes 4 servings

dinner

The question hovering on everyone's mind is
"What's for dessert?" We have the answer. In fact, we have
several answers. *black and gold marble cake*
(page 143) is the kind of old-fashioned layer cake
everyone yearns for. For pie lovers, there is the
coffee banana cream pie
(page 132). *cappuccino cheesecake ice*
cream dessert (page 147) is a special treat
for all. And, for a grand finale, we recommend the
exotic arabian coffee (page 141) or the
italian-style coffee (page 140).

two-layer mocha cheesecake

memorable mocha cake

mocha ribbon dessert

coffee banana cream pie

coffee butterscotch meringue pie

café mocha fruit tart

caffe latte bread pudding

coffee butterscotch sauce

saucy mocha pudding

tiramisu cheesecake

italian-style coffee

exotic arabian coffee

coffee chai

black and gold marble cake

cappuccino buttercream frosting

mocha frosting

coconut pecan frosting

cappuccino cheesecake ice cream dessert

coffee sugar cookies

iced caramel coffee

mexicali hot chocolate

mexican cream in tortilla cups

fruit salsa

coffee flan

two-layer
mocha cheesecake

A coffee cream cheese layer blankets a rich chocolate layer in this sophisticated cheesecake. Decorate each slice with a chocolate-covered coffee bean or a few chocolate curls.

Prep: 10 minutes • Bake: 40 minutes • Refrigerate: 3 hours

2 large eggs

2 tablespoons instant coffee

½ teaspoon vanilla extract

2 packages (8 ounces each) cream cheese, softened, divided

½ cup granulated sugar

4 squares (4 ounces) semi-sweet chocolate, melted, slightly cooled

1 prepared chocolate-flavor *or* graham cracker crumb crust (6 ounces *or* 9 inches)

✦ **HEAT** the oven to 350°F.

✦ **STIR** the eggs, instant coffee, and vanilla in a small bowl until well blended; set aside.

✦ **BEAT** the cream cheese and sugar in a large bowl with an electric mixer set on medium speed until well blended. Add the egg mixture and the melted chocolate and mix until blended. Reserve 1 cup of the cream cheese mixture; set aside. Add the melted chocolate to the remaining cream cheese mixture and mix until blended. Pour the mixture into the crust and spread evenly. Spoon the reserved coffee cream cheese mixture over the chocolate mixture and spread evenly.

✦ **BAKE** for 40 minutes or until the center is almost set. Cool completely on a wire rack.

✦ **REFRIGERATE** for at least 3 hours or overnight. Let stand at room temperature for 20 minutes before serving. Cut into slices to serve. Store the leftover cheesecake in the refrigerator.

Makes 8 servings

COFFEE HOUSE TIP

You can soften cream cheese quickly in the microwave. Place 1 completely unwrapped package of cream cheese in a microwavable bowl. Microwave on High for 15 seconds. Add 15 seconds for each additional package of cream cheese.

memorable
mocha cake

If you are looking for a great basic mocha cake recipe, look no further!
This one makes a marvelous birthday cake, too.

Prep: 15 minutes • Bake: 45 minutes

¾ cup (1½ sticks) butter *or* margarine

6 squares (6 ounces) semi-sweet chocolate

1½ cups granulated sugar

3 large eggs

2 teaspoons vanilla extract

2½ cups all-purpose flour, divided

1 teaspoon baking soda

¼ teaspoon salt

1½ cups room temperature brewed double-
    strength coffee

Coconut Pecan Frosting (page 145)

✦ **HEAT** the oven to 350°F. Lightly butter and flour a 13x9-inch baking pan.

✦ **MICROWAVE** the butter and chocolate in a large microwavable bowl on High for 2 minutes or until the butter has melted. Stir until the chocolate is completely melted.

✦ **STIR** the sugar into the chocolate until well blended. Beat in the eggs, 1 at a time, with an electric mixer set on low speed until completely mixed. Add the vanilla. Stir in ½ cup of the flour, the baking soda, and salt. Beat in the remaining 2 cups of flour alternately with the coffee until well blended and smooth. Pour the batter into the prepared pan.

✦ **BAKE** for 40 to 45 minutes or until a toothpick inserted in the center comes out clean. Cool completely on a wire rack. Frost with Coconut Pecan Frosting. Cut into squares to serve.

Makes 15 servings

COFFEE HOUSE TIP

This cake recipe can also be baked in two buttered and floured 9-inch round cake pans. The baking time will be about 35 minutes. Cool the cakes in their pans for 10 minutes before removing them from the pans to cool completely on wire racks.

mocha ribbon
dessert

A fudgy brownie forms the base of this mocha pudding dessert.
It is a fitting finale to a festive dinner.

Prep: 20 minutes • Bake: 25 minutes • Refrigerate: 4 hours

2 large eggs

3 tablespoons instant coffee, divided

1 teaspoon vanilla extract

¼ cup (½ stick) butter *or* margarine

4 squares (4 ounces) semi-sweet chocolate

¾ cup granulated sugar

½ cup all-purpose flour

½ cup chopped nuts

2 cups cold milk

2 packages (4-serving size each) vanilla *or* chocolate flavor instant pudding and pie filling

1 tub (8 ounces) frozen whipped topping, thawed

Chocolate curls, for garnish (page 20), (optional)

✦ **HEAT** the oven to 350°F. Line a 9-inch square baking pan with foil; lightly butter the foil.

✦ **STIR** the eggs, 1 tablespoon of the instant coffee, and vanilla in a small bowl until well blended; set aside.

✦ **MICROWAVE** the butter and chocolate in a large microwavable bowl on High for 2 minutes or until the butter has melted. Stir until the chocolate is completely melted.

✦ **STIR** the sugar into the chocolate mixture until well blended. Mix in the egg mixture. Stir in the flour and the nuts. Spread the batter in the prepared pan.

✦ **BAKE** for 20 to 25 minutes or until a toothpick inserted in the center comes out with fudgy crumbs. (Do not overbake.) Set the pan on a wire rack to cool completely.

✦ **STIR** the milk and the remaining 2 tablespoons of instant coffee in a large bowl until well blended. Add the pudding mixes. Beat with a wire whisk for 1 minute. Let stand for 2 minutes or until thickened. Spoon the mixture over the brownie in the pan. Spread the whipped topping over the pudding.

✦ **REFRIGERATE** for 4 hours or until ready to serve. Cut into squares to serve. Garnish with chocolate curls, if desired.

Makes 9 servings

mocha ribbon dessert

coffee banana cream pie

A mocha-flavored pudding makes this an exceptionally delicious banana cream pie.

Prep: 15 minutes • Cook: 10 minutes • Refrigerate: 4 hours

3 ½ cups milk

2 tablespoons instant coffee

2 packages (4-serving size each) chocolate
    flavor cook-and-serve pudding and pie
    filling

1 square (1 ounce) semi-sweet chocolate,
    coarsely chopped

1 large banana, sliced

1 baked pie crust, cooled (9 inch)

1 ½ cups thawed frozen whipped topping

+ **STIR** the milk and instant coffee in a medium
saucepan until well blended. Add the pudding
mixes and chocolate. Stirring constantly, cook on
medium heat until the mixture comes to a full
boil.

+ **ARRANGE** the banana slices in the prepared
crust. Pour the pudding mixture into the crust.
Cover the surface of the pie filling with the plastic
wrap.

+ **REFRIGERATE** for 4 hours or until firm. Spread
with the whipped topping. Cut into slices to serve.
Store the leftover pie in the refrigerator.

Makes 8 servings

COFFEE HOUSE INSPIRATION

Both of these pies are made using baked pie
crusts.

To make a perfect crust, be sure the oven is
preheated. Roll the pastry out on a floured
surface, using as little flour as possible to prevent the crust from becoming tough. Roll
from the center to the outside edges with
short, firm, strokes, changing directions reg-
ularly to achieve a circular shape.

To transfer the pastry easily to the pie plate,
fold half of the pastry over the rolling pin and
easily move it over the pie plate. Center the
crust so that the overhang is equal all around.
Press the crust gently into the pie plate. Trim
the overhang so that it extends about 1-inch
beyond the pie plate. Roll the edge of the
crust under and crimp it, if desired.

To keep the crust from shrinking when baking
an empty pie shell, place a large square of
wax paper in the pie shell and fill it with
uncooked rice, dried beans, or metal pie
weights.

coffee butterscotch
meringue pie

Airy meringue tops this luscious coffee-enhanced butterscotch pudding pie.

Prep: 20 minutes • Bake: 10 minutes • Refrigerate: 1 hour

3 ½ cups milk

2 tablespoons instant coffee

2 packages (4-serving size each) butterscotch flavor cook-and-serve pudding and pie filling

1 baked pie crust, cooled (9 inch)

3 large egg whites, at room temperature

¼ teaspoon cream of tartar

6 tablespoons granulated sugar

✦ **HEAT** the oven to 425°F.

✦ **STIR** the milk and instant coffee in a medium saucepan until well blended. Add the pudding mixes. Stirring constantly, cook on medium heat until the mixture comes to a full boil. Pour the pudding into the crust.

✦ **BEAT** the egg whites and the cream of tartar in a large bowl with an electric mixer set on high speed until foamy. Gradually add the sugar, 2 tablespoons at a time, beating until

stiff peaks form. Spread some meringue around the edge of the filling first, touching the crust all around, then fill in the center.

✦ **BAKE** for about 10 minutes or until the meringue is golden brown. Cool completely on a wire rack.

✦ **REFRIGERATE** 1 hour or until ready to serve. Cut into slices to serve.

Makes 8 servings

COFFEE HOUSE INSPIRATION

Instant coffee gives butterscotch pudding an intriguing flavor boost. Use this flavoring idea when you are preparing any pudding dessert.

café mocha
fruit tart

Frozen puff pastry is the secret to this beautiful tart.
Coffee flavors the cream cheese filling and fresh fruit completes the picture.

Prep: 20 minutes • Bake: 15 minutes

½ package (1 sheet) frozen puff pastry sheets

1 tablespoon milk

2 teaspoons instant coffee

1 package (8 ounces) cream cheese, softened

⅓ cup powdered sugar

3 cups assorted cut-up fruit, such as sliced strawberries, raspberries, blackberries, blueberries, mandarin oranges, sliced peeled kiwi

2 tablespoons currant jelly, melted, cooled

+ **HEAT** the oven to 400°F.

+ **THAW** the puff pastry sheet at room temperature for 30 minutes. Unfold the pastry on a lightly floured surface. Roll the pastry into a 14x10-inch rectangle. Place the pastry on a large baking sheet. Brush the edges of the rectangle with water. Fold over ½ inch on all sides and press firmly to form a rim. Pierce the pastry thoroughly with a fork.

+ **BAKE** for 15 minutes or until golden (after 10 minutes of baking, break any large air bubbles with a fork). Cool completely on a wire rack.

+ **STIR** the milk and instant coffee in a small bowl until well blended; set aside.

+ **BEAT** the cream cheese and powdered sugar in a medium bowl until well blended. Mix in the milk mixture until well blended. Spread the mixture in the puff pastry shell. Top with the fruit. Brush the melted jelly over the fruit just before serving. Serve immediately or cover and refrigerate for up to 4 hours. Cut into squares to serve.

Makes 12 servings

COFFEE HOUSE INSPIRATION

If you love desserts made with puff pastry, try our *coffee napoleons with strawberries* (page 102).

café mocha fruit tart

caffe latte bread pudding

This simple bread pudding is studded with chunks of semi-sweet and white chocolate.

Prep: 15 minutes • Bake: 40 minutes

1 ½ cups milk

1 cup cold brewed strong coffee

1 package (4-serving size) vanilla flavor cook-
and-serve pudding and pie filling

3 cups French bread cubes

2 squares (2 ounces) semi-sweet chocolate,
chopped

2 squares (2 ounces) white chocolate, chopped

1 teaspoon vanilla extract

½ teaspoon ground cinnamon

+ **HEAT** the oven to 375°F.

+ **POUR** the milk and coffee into a large bowl. Stir
in the pudding mix until well blended. Stir in the
bread cubes, chocolates, vanilla, and cinnamon.
Pour the mixture into a 1-quart baking dish.

+ **BAKE** for 40 minutes or until the mixture comes
to a boil. Remove the dish from the oven. Let stand
for 10 minutes before serving. Serve warm. Spoon
into dessert dishes to serve.

Makes 6 servings

coffee butterscotch sauce

The flavor of coffee perfectly balances the sweetness of this sauce.

Prep: 5 minutes • Cook: 5 minutes

¾ cup firmly packed brown sugar

½ cup granulated sugar

½ cup evaporated milk

3 tablespoons butter *or* margarine

2 tablespoons corn syrup

1 tablespoon instant coffee

1 teaspoon vanilla extract

+ **MIX** the sugars, milk, butter, corn syrup, and
instant coffee in a small saucepan. Bring the
mixture to a boil over low heat, stirring constantly.

+ **COOK** slowly for 3 minutes, stirring frequently.
Remove from the heat and stir in the vanilla. Serve
warm. Store the leftover sauce in the refrigerator.

Makes about 1½ cups sauce

saucy mocha
pudding

After a tough day in the real world, here's a dessert that will warm up

your heart and soul. It's a baked mocha pudding with a cakey bottom.

Coffee and a hint of cinnamon add interest.

Prep: 10 minutes • Bake: 50 minutes

1 package (2-layer size) chocolate cake mix

2 cups cold brewed strong coffee, divided

2 cups cold milk

2 packages (4-serving size each) chocolate
    flavor instant pudding and pie filling

⅓ cup granulated sugar

¼ teaspoon ground cinnamon

+ **HEAT** the oven to 350°F. Lightly butter a 13x9-inch baking pan.

+ **PREPARE** the cake mix as directed on the package, substituting 1 cup of the coffee for the water. Pour the batter into the prepared pan.

+ **STIR** the remaining 1 cup of coffee and the milk in a large bowl until well blended. Add the pudding mixes sugar, and cinnamon. Beat with an electric mixer set on low speed for 1 to 2 minutes or until well blended. Pour the mixture over the cake batter in the pan.

+ **BAKE** for 45 to 50 minutes or until a toothpick inserted in the center comes out clean. Serve warm. Spoon into dessert dishes to serve.

Makes 12 servings

tiramisu
cheesecake

Ladyfingers form the crust of this easy-to-make cheesecake variation of the popular Italian recipe. (See the classic version on page 169.)

Prep: 15 minutes • Bake: 40 minutes • Refrigerate: 3 hours

1 package (3 ounces) soft ladyfingers, split

½ cup room temperature brewed double-strength coffee, divided

2 packages (8 ounces each) cream cheese, softened

½ cup granulated sugar

2 large eggs

Whipped cream and chocolate twigs for garnish (optional)

+ **HEAT** the oven to 350°F.

+ **ARRANGE** the ladyfingers on the bottom and up the sides of a 9-inch pie plate, cutting as necessary so that the ladyfingers line the pie plate. Brush the ladyfingers with ¼ cup of the coffee.

+ **BEAT** the cream cheese and sugar in a large bowl with an electric mixer set on medium speed until well blended. Mix in the eggs and the remaining ¼ cup of coffee until well blended. Pour the mixture into the ladyfinger crust.

+ **BAKE** for 35 to 40 minutes or until the center is almost set. Cool the cheesecake completely on a wire rack.

+ **REFRIGERATE** for at least 3 hours or overnight. Garnish with whipped cream and chocolate twigs, if desired. Cut into slices to serve. Store the leftover cheesecake in the refrigerator.

Makes 8 servings

A DROP OF HISTORY

1901   On August 27, Joel Cheek and John Neal form the Nashville Coffee and Manufacturing Company and begin to manufacture Maxwell House coffee at the company's plant on 148 North Market Street in Nashville, Tennessee.

tiramisu cheesecake

italian-style coffee

The bold tastes of anise seed and lemon peel distinguish this coffee.

Prep: 5 minutes

½ cup ground coffee

1 tablespoon grated lemon peel

1 teaspoon anise seed

2 to 4 tablespoons granulated sugar

3 cups cold water

Strips of lemon peel, for garnish (optional)

◆ **PLACE** the coffee, grated lemon peel, and anise seed in the filter in the brew basket of a coffee maker. Place the sugar into the empty pot of the coffee maker.

◆ **PREPARE** the coffee with the cold water. When the brewing is complete, stir until well mixed. Pour into demitasse cups or other small cups. Garnish each cup with a strip of lemon peel, if desired.

Makes 8 servings

ENTERTAINING IDEA

For an unusual ending to a dinner party, offer an international selection of coffees to go with dessert. Choose from the recipes on these two pages to get you started. Or select from some of these other coffee beverages: *chocolate cherry coffee* (page 181), *café au lait* (page 28), *spiced brazilian chocolate* (page 121), *thai coffee* (page 93), or *tropical frappé* (page 181).

exotic arabian coffee

This hot coffee will transform the evening into an Arabian night.

Prep: 5 minutes

½ cup ground coffee

½ teaspoon ground cinnamon

¼ to ½ teaspoon ground cardamom

2 tablespoons honey

3 cups cold water

✦ **PLACE** the coffee, cinnamon, and cardamom in the filter in the brew basket of a coffee maker. Pour the honey into the empty pot of the coffee maker.

✦ **PREPARE** the coffee with the cold water. When the brewing is complete, stir until well mixed. Pour into demitasse cups or other small cups.

Makes about 8 demitasse servings or 3 cups

coffee chai

This is a coffee version of a favorite ethnic spiced tea beverage.

Prep: 10 minutes • Stand: 10 minutes

4 cups milk

¼ cup instant coffee

¼ cup firmly packed brown sugar

2 cinnamon sticks, broken

¼ teaspoon ground cardamom *or*
2 cardamom pods

⅛ teaspoon ground allspice

✦ **MIX** all the ingredients in a large saucepan. Simmer for 5 minutes over low heat, stirring occasionally. Let stand for 10 minutes. Strain. Pour into large cups or mugs.

Makes 6 servings

COFFEE HOUSE INSPIRATION

Cool Variation: Prepare the coffee as directed and refrigerate for a cold beverage. Serve over ice.

black and gold marble cake

Marble cake is an old-fashioned gem that's well worth rediscovering.
This two-layer cake makes a spectacular presentation.

Prep: 20 minutes • Bake: 35 minutes

3 tablespoons hot water

2 tablespoons instant coffee

2 squares (2 ounces) unsweetened chocolate, melted

1²/₃ cups plus 2 tablespoons granulated sugar, divided

³/₄ teaspoon baking soda, divided

2 cups all-purpose flour

1½ teaspoons baking powder

1 teaspoon salt

³/₄ cup butter, at room temperature

1 cup buttermilk

1 teaspoon vanilla extract

3 large eggs

Mocha Frosting (recipe on page 145)

+ **HEAT** the oven to 350°F. Lightly butter and flour two 9-inch round cake pans.

+ **STIR** the water and instant coffee in a small bowl until well blended. Stir in the melted chocolate and 2 tablespoons of the sugar until well blended. Stir in ¼ teaspoon of the baking soda until well mixed; set aside. Mix the flour, remaining 1²/₃ cups of sugar, baking powder, remaining ½ teaspoon of baking soda, and salt in a medium bowl; set aside.

+ **BEAT** the butter in a large bowl with an electric mixer set on medium speed until light and fluffy. Gradually add the flour mixture, buttermilk, and vanilla and beat for 2 minutes, scraping the bowl occasionally. Add the eggs and beat 1 minute longer. Pour half of the batter into another bowl and stir in the chocolate mixture until well blended. Spoon the plain and chocolate batters alternately into the two prepared pans. Cut through the batters with a knife or spatula to marbleize.

+ **BAKE** for 30 to 35 minutes or until the cakes spring back when lightly touched. Cool the cakes in the pans for 10 minutes. Remove the cakes from the pans and cool completely on wire racks. Frost with Mocha Frosting. Cut into slices to serve.

Makes 12 servings

black and gold marble cake
with mocha frosting (page 145)

cappuccino buttercream frosting

This recipe is especially delicious on the Coffee Brownies (page 172),
but give it a try on your favorite cake or cupcakes, too.

Prep: 10 minutes

1 envelope instant cappuccino mix, any flavor
¼ cup hot milk
½ cup (1 stick) butter *or* margarine, softened
1 package (16 ounces) powdered sugar

✦ **STIR** the cappuccino mix and hot milk in a small bowl until well blended.

✦ **BEAT** the butter, powdered sugar, and cappuccino mixture in a large bowl with an electric mixer set on low speed until well blended and smooth. Let stand, if necessary, until the frosting is of spreading consistency.

Makes about 2 ½ cups frosting *or* enough to frost one 13x9-inch pan of brownies or cake, *or* 24 cupcakes

COFFEE HOUSE TIP

FROSTING A CAKE LIKE A PRO:

✦ Cool cakes thoroughly before frosting. Gently brush off any loose crumbs. To make the frosting easier, place the cake on a lazy susan or a bowl which is turned upside down. You can easily turn the cake as you frost it.

✦ Using a cake spatula, start frosting a cake by beginning on the top and ending with the sides. When the frosting is as thick and even as you want it to be, smooth the top edge of the cake with the cake spatula. Hold the spatula at an angle and spread the frosting in toward the center of the cake.

✦ In some cases, you might want to start with a "crumb coat." A crumb coat holds in any loose crumbs of frosting. Apply a thin layer of frosting and let it set for about 15 minutes in the refrigerator. Then you will be able to flawlessly apply a second coat over the cake.

mocha frosting

The simple addition of instant coffee gives chocolate frosting a sophisticated flair.

Prep: 10 minutes

3 tablespoons milk

2 tablespoons instant coffee

1 teaspoon vanilla extract

½ cup (1 stick) butter, softened

1 package (16 ounces) powdered sugar

2 squares (2 ounces) unsweetened chocolate, melted

✦ **STIR** the milk, coffee, and vanilla in a small bowl until well blended, set aside.

✦ **BEAT** the butter in a large bowl with an electric mixer set on medium speed until fluffy. Gradually beat in the powdered sugar, milk mixture, and melted chocolate until well blended and smooth.

Makes about 2 cups frosting *or* enough to fill and frost two 9-inch round cake layers

COFFEE HOUSE INSPIRATION

For a simple coffee-flavored frosting, just omit the chocolate in this recipe.

coconut pecan frosting

This frosting is delicious on the Marvelous Mocha Cake (page 129).

Prep: 20 minutes

⅔ cup (5.33 fluid ounce can) evaporated milk

⅔ cup granulated sugar

2 large egg yolks, lightly beaten

⅓ cup butter *or* margarine

1 teaspoon vanilla extract

1 cup sweetened flaked coconut

⅔ cup chopped pecans

✦ **MIX** the milk, sugar, egg yolks, butter, and vanilla in a medium saucepan. Cook and stir on medium heat for about 10 minutes until the mixture thickens. Remove the pan from the heat.

✦ **STIR** in the coconut and pecans. Cool to room temperature and until of spreading consistency.

Makes about 2 cups frosting, *or* enough to frost one 13x9-inch cake *or* cover the tops of two 9-inch round cake layers.

cappuccino
cheesecake
ice cream dessert

Make this easy layered dessert with your favorite flavor of cappuccino mix.

Prep: 20 minutes • Freeze: 4 hours

1 package (11.1 ounces) no-bake dessert real
   cheesecake

2 envelopes instant cappuccino mix, any flavor
   divided

2 tablespoons granulated sugar

6 tablespoons butter *or* margarine, melted

1 tablespoon water

1½ cups cold milk

1 tub (8 ounces) frozen whipped topping,
   thawed

Chocolate topping for serving with the
   dessert (optional)

✦ **LINE** a 9x5-inch loaf pan with aluminum foil so
that the foil extends 2 inches beyond the two long
sides of the pan.

✦ **STIR** the crust mix from the cheesecake, 1 envelope of the cappuccino mix, sugar, butter, and
water thoroughly in a medium bowl until the
crumbs are well moistened. Press ½ cup of the
mixture firmly onto the bottom of the prepared
pan; reserve the remaining crumb mixture.

✦ **BEAT** the milk, cheesecake filling mix, and

remaining 1 envelope of cappuccino mix in a
medium bowl with an electric mixer set on low
speed until blended. Beat on medium speed for
3 minutes. (The filling will be thick.) Gently stir
in the whipped topping. Spoon one-third of the
mixture over the crust in the pan. Top with
one-third of the reserved crumb mixture. Repeat
the layers, ending with the crumb mixture.

✦ **FREEZE** for at least 4 hours or overnight. Lift the
dessert from the pan, using the foil as handles. Let
stand at room temperature for about 10 minutes or
until the dessert can be sliced easily. Garnish as
desired. Cut into slices. Serve with the chocolate
topping, if desired. Store the leftover dessert in the
freezer.

Makes 12 servings

COFFEE HOUSE INSPIRATION

**Use your creativity when garnishing this
dessert. Chocolate curls, raspberries and/or
sliced strawberries, drizzled melted
chocolate, chocolate-covered coffee
beans—the choice is yours.**

cappuccino cheesecake ice cream dessert

coffee
sugar cookies

Sugar cookies with a kiss of coffee are the perfect ending

to a simple supper.

Prep: 20 minutes plus refrigerating • Bake: 12 minutes

2 large eggs

1 tablespoon instant coffee

1 teaspoon vanilla extract

2 cups all-purpose flour

½ teaspoon baking soda

¼ teaspoon ground cinnamon

¼ teaspoon salt

1 cup (2 sticks) butter *or* margarine

1¼ cups sugar, divided

+ **HEAT** the oven to 375°F.

+ **STIR** the eggs, coffee, and vanilla in a small bowl until well blended; set aside. Mix the flour, baking soda, cinnamon, and salt in a small bowl; set aside.

+ **BEAT** the butter and 1 cup of the sugar in a large bowl with an electric mixer set on medium speed until light and fluffy. Beat in the egg mixture. Gradually add the flour mixture, beating well after each addition. Cover with plastic wrap.

+ **REFRIGERATE** for 1½ hours. Shape into 1-inch balls. Roll in the remaining sugar. Place on un-greased baking sheets.

+ **BAKE** for 10 to 12 minutes or until the edges are lightly browned. Remove the cookies from the baking sheets. Cool completely on wire racks. Store in a tightly covered container.

Makes about 4 dozen cookies

COFFEE HOUSE INSPIRATION

For crisper cookies, flatten each ball of cookie dough to ¼-inch thickness using the bottom of a glass. Decrease the baking time to 8 to 10 minutes.

iced caramel coffee

Cool, sweet, and creamy, this iced coffee can serve as dessert.

Prep: 10 minutes

1 cup half-and-half
¼ cup water
¼ cup caramel dessert topping
1 to 2 tablespoons instant coffee
½ teaspoon vanilla extract
Ice cubes
Whipped cream (optional)

✦ **PLACE** the half-and-half, water, dessert topping, instant coffee, and vanilla in a blender container; cover. Blend on high speed until smooth. Serve over ice in tall glasses. Top with whipped cream, if desired. Serve immediately.

Makes 2 servings

mexicali hot chocolate

Cinnamon and chocolate make this a great beverage to top off a spicy meal.

Prep: 10 minutes

½ cup heavy (whipping) cream
1 square (1 ounce) semi-sweet baking
  chocolate, coarsely chopped
2 cups hot freshly brewed strong coffee
2 tablespoons granulated sugar
½ teaspoon ground cinnamon
Whipped cream (optional)

✦ **PLACE** the cream and chocolate in a medium saucepan. Stirring constantly, heat over very low heat until the chocolate is melted.

✦ **MIX** the coffee, sugar, and cinnamon. Stir into the chocolate mixture until well blended. Pour into large cups or mugs. Sweeten to taste and serve with whipped cream, if desired. Serve immediately.

Makes 4 servings

COFFEE HOUSE INSPIRATION

Cool Variation: Prepare as directed and refrigerate. Serve over ice.

mexican cream
in tortilla cups

This fun dessert makes a splendid ending to a Mexican meal—or to any meal! Flour tortillas are lightly brushed with butter, sprinkled with cinnamon sugar, and baked into cups to hold a delectable coffee cream. Serve with Fruit Salsa (following page) to complete the Mexican theme.

Prep: 20 minutes • Bake: 15 minutes • Refrigerate: 1 hour

TORTILLA CUPS:

2 tablespoons granulated sugar

1 teaspoon ground cinnamon

6 flour tortillas (8 inch)

2 tablespoons butter *or* margarine, melted

COFFEE CREAM:

1 cup cold half-and-half *or* milk

1 tablespoon instant coffee

1 package (4-serving size) vanilla *or* white
   chocolate flavor pudding and pie filling

1 tub (8 ounces) frozen whipped topping,
   thawed

Sliced star fruit, additional whipped topping and
   raspberry sauce, for garnish (optional)

Fruit Salsa (following page)

PREPARE THE TORTILLA CUPS:

✦ **HEAT** the oven to 400°F.

✦ **MIX** the sugar and cinnamon. Soften the tortillas

as directed on the package. Brush 1 side of each tortilla with the melted butter and sprinkle this side evenly with the sugar mixture. Gently press each tortilla, buttered side facing out, into a 10-ounce custard cup to form the tortilla into a cup.

✦ **BAKE** for 15 minutes or until crisp. Remove the tortillas from the custard cups. Cool completely on a wire rack.

PREPARE THE COFFEE CREAM:

✦ **STIR** the half-and-half and instant coffee in a large bowl until well blended. Add the pudding mix. Beat with a wire whisk for 1 minute. Let stand for 5 minutes. Gently stir in the whipped topping.

✦ **REFRIGERATE** for 1 hour or until ready to serve. Just before serving, fill the tortilla cups with the coffee cream. Garnish with star fruit, whipped topping, and raspberry sauce, if desired. Serve with Fruit Salsa.

Makes 6 servings

*mexican cream in tortilla cups
with fruit salsa (page 152)*

fruit salsa

This easy fresh berry salsa makes a colorful, flavorful topping for many desserts.

Prep: 5 minutes plus refrigeration time

1 pint strawberries, sliced or quartered
1 pint blueberries
½ pint raspberries

♦ **MIX** the strawberries, blueberries, and raspberries in a medium bowl.

♦ **REFRIGERATE** until ready to serve.

Makes about 4 cups

COFFEE HOUSE TIP

A garnish that would be delicious on these desserts or beverages is toasted coconut. To keep the toasted coconut crisp, sprinkle it on just before serving. Toasting the coconut also adds extra flavor. Spread the coconut in a shallow pan. Toast at 350°F for 7 to 12 minutes or until lightly browned, stirring frequently. Or, toast in a microwave oven on High for 5 minutes for 1⅓ cups of coconut, stirring several times. Cool before sprinkling on desserts or beverages. Store in a tightly covered container in the freezer until ready to use.

ENTERTAINING IDEA

Have a Mexican Dessert Fiesta. Decorate with brightly colored Mexican flowers and piñatas. Serve the *coffee flan* (page 153), *mexican cream* (page 151) with *fruit salsa*, and *coffee ice cream* with *mexican chocolate sauce* (page 195). Both hot and iced coffee beverages such as *mexicali hot chocolate* and *iced caramel coffee* (page 149) would make delicious accompaniments.

coffee flan

Flan is a favorite Latin American custard dessert.
Coffee is the ideal counterpoint to its creamy sweetness.

Prep: 15 minutes • Bake: 1 hour • Refrigerate: 2 hours

1 ¼ cups granulated sugar, divided

3 ½ cups milk

2 tablespoons instant coffee

5 large eggs, well beaten

1 teaspoon vanilla extract

¼ teaspoon salt

+ **HEAT** the oven to 325°F.

+ **STIRRING** constantly, heat ¾ cup of the sugar in a small saucepan on low heat until the sugar is melted and golden brown. Remove the pan from the heat. Carefully pour the melted sugar into a 9-inch round cake pan, tilting the pan to evenly coat the bottom.

+ **STIR** the milk and instant coffee in a medium bowl until well blended; set aside.

+ **BEAT** the eggs, the remaining ½ cup of sugar, vanilla, and salt in a large bowl until well blended. Stir in the milk mixture until well blended. Pour this mixture into the caramel-coated pan. Place the cake pan in a larger baking pan and place it on the center rack in the oven. Fill the larger pan with hot water so that the water comes 1 inch up the side of the pan.

+ **BAKE** for 50 to 60 minutes or until a knife inserted 1 inch from the edge comes out clean. Carefully remove the cake pan from the larger pan. Cool on a wire rack for 1 hour.

+ **REFRIGERATE** for 2 hours or until ready to serve. To unmold, run a small metal spatula around the edge of the custard. Invert the flan onto a serving plate; shake slightly to loosen. Carefully remove the pan. Cut the flan into slices.

Makes 8 servings

after the show

Whether you have spent the evening out at the theatre or have just watched a video until the last credits have faded from the television screen, there usually comes a yearning for something sweet to eat. *coffee caramel nut tart* (page 171) might fit the bill. Or perhaps the *coffee chocolate cheesecake* (page 158) could be just the thing for those who adore both cheesecake and chocolate.

This chapter ends with some new ideas for drinks, like *toffee coffee,* *chocolate cherry coffee* and *tropical frappé,* (pages 180-181)—to be served with sweetened whipped cream and fancy chocolate curls.

intensely mocha mousse cake
divine decadence
coffee chocolate cheesecake
coconut candy bar pie
caribbean fudge pie
tuxedo ladyfinger dessert
mississippi mud pie
mocha passion
awesome sundae pie
chocolate lover's cheesecake
tiramisu
coffee caramel nut tart
coffee brownies
easy mocha fondue
café caramel fondue
petite mocha cakes
easy truffles
bittersweet coffee glaze
chocolate mousse coffee
cappuccino cookie roll
vanilla coffee
toffee coffee
tropical frappé
chocolate cherry coffee

intensely mocha
mousse cake

This flourless cake will make an unforgettable impression on any chocolate lover.

Prep: 15 minutes • Bake: 45 minutes • Refrigerate: 4 hours

9 squares (9 ounces) bittersweet chocolate,
   coarsely chopped

¾ cup cold brewed strong coffee

½ cup granulated sugar

½ cup corn syrup

¼ cup (½ stick) butter *or* margarine,
   cut into tablespoons

¼ cup cornstarch

¼ teaspoon salt

3 large eggs, at room temperature, lightly beaten

1 cup heavy (whipping) cream

Boiling water

Softly whipped cream and sliced strawberries
   or raspberries, for garnish (optional)

✦ **HEAT** the oven to 350°F. Lightly butter and flour a 9-inch springform pan.

✦ **MICROWAVE** the chocolate, coffee, sugar, corn syrup, and butter in a large microwavable bowl on High for 2 minutes or until the butter has melted. Stir until the chocolate is completely melted. Stir in the cornstarch and salt until smooth. Refrigerate for 5 minutes, stirring occasionally, until the mixture has cooled (it may still be warm to the touch).

✦ **WHISK** the eggs into the chocolate mixture. Beat the cream in a chilled large bowl with an electric mixer set on medium speed until soft peaks form. (Do not overbeat.) Gently stir the whipped cream into the chocolate mixture. Pour the mixture into the prepared pan. Place the pan in a larger roasting pan and place it on the center rack in the oven. Fill the roasting pan with boiling water so that the water comes halfway up the sides of the springform pan.

✦ **BAKE** for 45 minutes or until the mixture is just set. The top will feel lightly firm to the touch. Carefully remove the springform pan from the water bath. Cool on a wire rack. Cover the top with plastic wrap.

✦ **REFRIGERATE** for 4 hours or until ready to serve. See Tip below for easy serving. Garnish with whipped cream and sliced berries, if desired.

Makes 8 servings

COFFEE HOUSE TIP

To serve this cake, run a thin knife around the edge of the springform pan and then carefully release and remove the form. Using a large, sharp knife, cut the cake into 8 slices, wiping the blade of the knife after each cut. Using a pie server, serve the slices of cake.

divine decadence

Coffee adds a boost of flavor to this dense single-layer fudgy cake.
A shiny mocha glaze shows off its charms.

Prep: 15 minutes • Bake: 45 minutes

CAKE:

5 squares (5 ounces) semi-sweet chocolate,
  divided
½ cup corn syrup
½ cup (1 stick) butter *or* margarine
2 tablespoons instant coffee
¾ cup granulated sugar
3 large eggs
1 teaspoon vanilla extract
1 cup all-purpose flour
1 cup chopped walnuts

GLAZE:

1 teaspoon instant coffee
1 teaspoon milk
3 squares (3 ounces) semi-sweet chocolate
1 tablespoon butter
2 tablespoons corn syrup

PREPARE THE CAKE:

✦ **HEAT** the oven to 350°F. Lightly butter and flour a 9-inch round cake pan.

✦ **MICROWAVE** the chocolate, corn syrup, butter, and instant coffee in a large microwavable bowl on High for 2 minutes or until the butter is melted. Stir until the chocolate is completely melted.

✦ **STIR** the sugar into the chocolate mixture until well blended. Mix in the eggs and vanilla. Gradually stir in the flour and walnuts until well blended. Pour the batter into the prepared pan.

✦ **BAKE** for 40 to 45 minutes or until a toothpick inserted in the center comes out clean. (Do not overbake.) Set the pan on a wire rack to cool for 10 minutes. Loosen the cake from the sides of the pan with a knife or spatula. Gently invert the cake onto the rack. Cool completely.

PREPARE THE GLAZE:

✦ **STIR** the instant coffee and milk in a small bowl until well blended; set aside.

✦ **MICROWAVE** the chocolate and butter in a medium microwavable bowl on High for 1½ to 2 minutes or until the chocolate is almost melted. Stir until the chocolate is completely melted. Stir in the corn syrup and coffee mixture until well blended. Spread the glaze evenly over the top and sides of the cake. Let stand for 1 hour or until the glaze is set. Cut into slices to serve.

Makes 8 servings

coffee chocolate cheesecake

*A chocolate cookie crust is given a rich mocha cream cheese
filling and covered with a glossy chocolate glaze.*

Prep: 20 minutes • Bake: 50 minutes • Refrigerate: 3 hours

CRUST:

1 ⅓ cups chocolate wafer cookie crumbs

⅓ cup butter *or* margarine, melted

FILLING:

3 large eggs

3 tablespoons instant coffee

2 packages (8 ounces each) cream cheese,
   softened

1 cup granulated sugar

8 squares (8 ounces) semi-sweet chocolate,
   melted

½ cup sour cream

GLAZE:

½ cup heavy (whipping) cream

1 tablespoon instant coffee

4 squares (4 ounces) semi-sweet chocolate

Chocolate curls, for garnish (optional)

PREPARE THE CRUST:

✦ **HEAT** the oven to 350°F.

✦ **MIX** the crumbs and butter in a small bowl. Press
   the mixture evenly onto the bottom of a 9-inch
   round springform pan. Refrigerate while preparing
   the filling

PREPARE THE FILLING:

✦ **STIR** the eggs and instant coffee in a small bowl
   until well blended; set aside.

✦ **BEAT** the cream cheese and sugar in a large
   bowl with an electric mixer set on medium speed
   until well blended. Add the egg mixture and mix
   until blended. Beat in the melted chocolate and
   the sour cream. Pour the mixture over the crust.

✦ **BAKE** for 40 to 50 minutes or until the center is
   almost set. Run a knife or a metal spatula around
   the edge of the pan. Cool the cheesecake
   completely on a wire rack. Refrigerate for at least 3
   hours or overnight.

PREPARE THE GLAZE:

✦ **STIR** the cream and instant coffee in a medium
   microwavable bowl until well blended. Add the
   chocolate.

✦ **MICROWAVE** on High for 2 minutes, stirring
   halfway through cooking time. Stir until the chocolate is completely melted and the mixture is smooth.
   Spoon the glaze evenly over the cheesecake.

✦ **REFRIGERATE** for 1 hour or until ready to serve.
   Garnish with chocolate curls, if desired. Cut into
   slices to serve.

Makes 16 servings

coffee chocolate cheesecake

coconut candy bar pie

This pie contains all the flavors of our favorite candy bars.
A buttery coconut and pecan crust is filled with a chocolate cream
cheese mixture subtly accented with a hint of coffee.

Prep: 15 minutes • Bake: 20 minutes • Freeze: 4 hours

2 cups sweetened flaked coconut

½ cup chopped pecans

¼ cup (½ stick) butter *or* margarine, melted

⅓ cup milk, divided

2 tablespoons instant coffee

4 squares (4 ounces) semi-sweet chocolate

4 ounces cream cheese, softened

¼ cup granulated sugar

1 tub (8 ounces) frozen whipped topping, thawed

✦ **HEAT** the oven to 350°F. Butter a 9-inch pie plate.

✦ **MIX** the coconut, pecans, and butter in a medium bowl. Press the mixture evenly on the bottom and side of the pie plate. Bake for 20 minutes or until lightly browned. Cool completely on a wire rack.

✦ **STIR** 2 tablespoons of the milk and the instant coffee in a large microwavable bowl until well blended. Add the chocolate. Microwave on High for 1½ minutes or until the chocolate is almost melted, stirring halfway through the cooking time. Stir until the chocolate is completely melted.

✦ **BEAT** in the cream cheese, sugar, and remaining milk with a wire whisk until well blended. Refrigerate for about 10 minutes to cool. Gently stir in the whipped topping until smooth. Spoon the mixture into the crust.

✦ **FREEZE** for 4 hours or until firm. Let stand at room temperature for 15 minutes. Dip the bottom of the pie plate in hot water for 30 seconds for easy cutting and serving. Cut into slices to serve. Store the leftover pie in the freezer.

Makes 8 servings

COFFEE HOUSE INSPIRATION

A fun and unusual garnish for desserts and beverages is Piped Chocolate Shapes. Place 1 square (1 ounce) of semi-sweet or bittersweet chocolate in a freezer-weight zipper-style plastic bag. Close the bag tightly. Microwave on High for about 1 minute or until the chocolate is melted. Tightly fold down the top of the bag and snip off a tiny piece of one corner (about ⅛ inch). Line a baking sheet with wax paper. Draw a design on the wax paper, if desired (see the coffee cup shape on page 174 and 187). Drizzle the chocolate to trace the shapes or drizzle it into free-form designs. Refrigerate the chocolate shapes for about 30 minutes or until firm. Carefully remove the shapes from the wax paper. Place on the desserts or beverages, or store in a tightly covered container in the freezer until ready to use.

caribbean fudge pie

*Serve this moist, dense pie with a scoop of vanilla ice cream on top
and accompanied by a tall glass of iced coffee.*

Prep: 20 minutes • Bake: 25 minutes • Refrigerate: 1 hour

8 squares (8 ounces) semi-sweet chocolate

¼ cup (½ stick) butter *or* margarine, softened

¾ cup firmly packed brown sugar

3 large eggs

1 tablespoon instant coffee

1 tablespoon dark rum *or* 1 teaspoon rum
    extract *or* 1 teaspoon vanilla extract

¼ cup all-purpose flour

1 cup chopped walnuts

1 unbaked pie crust (9 inch)

½ cup walnut halves *or* pieces

Whipped cream *or* ice cream (optional)

◆ **HEAT** the oven to 375°F.

◆ **MICROWAVE** the chocolate in a large
microwavable bowl on High for 2 minutes or until
almost melted, stirring every minute. Stir until
completely melted.

◆ **BEAT** the butter and brown sugar in a large bowl
until light and fluffy. Add the eggs, 1 at a time,
beating well after each addition. Mix in the melted
chocolate, instant coffee, and rum until blended.
Stir in the flour and chopped walnuts. Pour the
mixture into the crust. Decorate the top of the pie
with the walnut halves.

◆ **BAKE** in the lower third of the oven for 25 minutes
or until set. Cool completely on a wire rack. Cut
into slices. Top with the whipped cream or serve
with ice cream, if desired.

Makes 10 servings

tuxedo ladyfinger
dessert

Little ladyfingers dressed up in tuxedos make this dessert a black-tie affair.

Prep: 20 minutes • Refrigerate: 1 hour

TUXEDO LADYFINGERS:

4 squares (4 ounces) semi-sweet chocolate

8 hard ladyfingers

Melted white chocolate, for garnish
  (optional)

CREAMY DESSERTS:

1 package (8 ounces) cream cheese, softened

¾ cup room temperature freshly brewed
  double-strength coffee, divided

1 cup cold milk

1 package (4-serving size) vanilla flavor
  instant pudding and pie filling

1 tub (8 ounces) frozen whipped topping,
  thawed, divided

Grated chocolate, for garnish (optional)

PREPARE THE TUXEDO LADYFINGERS:

✦ MELT the chocolate as directed on the package.
Dip the ladyfingers into the chocolate, covering
at least half of each ladyfinger in a V-shape. Let the
excess chocolate drip off. Place the ladyfingers on a
wax paper-lined tray. Using the melted white chocolate,
pipe small dots onto the ladyfingers to create
buttons. Let stand at room temperature or
refrigerate for 30 minutes or until the chocolate is firm.

tuxedo ladyfinger dessert

PREPARE THE CREAMY DESSERTS:

✦ BEAT the cream cheese and coffee in a large bowl
  with a wire whisk until smooth. Gradually beat in
  the cold milk until smooth. Add the pudding mix.
  Beat with the wire whisk for 1 minute. Gently stir
  in 2 cups of the whipped topping. Spoon the
  mixture into 8 coffee cups or dessert dishes.

✦ REFRIGERATE for 1 hour or until ready to serve.
  Top with the remaining whipped topping. Garnish
  with grated chocolate, if desired. Serve with the
  Tuxedo Ladyfingers.

Makes 8 servings

COFFEE HOUSE INSPIRATION

**For an easy trifle-like dessert, layer this
filling with pound cake cubes and sliced
strawberries in a trifle or other large bowl.
Garnish with the remaining whipped topping and whole berries. Refrigerate until
ready to serve.**

mississippi
mud pie

Fudge sauce forms the gooey layer of "mud" on the bottom of this frozen pie.

Prep: 10 minutes • Freeze: 6 hours

1 cup fudge sauce, divided

1 prepared chocolate flavor crumb crust
(6 ounces or 9 inches)

1½ cups cold half-and-half *or* milk

1 package (4-serving size) vanilla flavor
instant pudding and pie filling

1 envelope instant cappuccino mix, any flavor

1 tub (8 ounces) frozen whipped topping,
thawed

✦ **SPREAD** ½ cup of the fudge sauce on the bottom of the crust.

✦ **POUR** the cold half-and-half into a large bowl. Add the pudding and cappuccino mixes. Beat with a wire whisk for 1 minute. Let stand for 5 minutes. Gently stir in the whipped topping. Spoon the mixture into the crust.

✦ **FREEZE** for 6 hours or overnight until firm. Let stand at room temperature for about 10 minutes or until the pie can be cut easily. Cut into slices to serve. Serve with the remaining ½ cup fudge sauce. Store the leftover pie in the freezer.

Makes 8 servings

mocha passion

Our directions tell you how to create one spectacular and mouth-watering centerpiece dessert, but you can also make this recipe as eight individual servings.

Prep: 15 minutes

Coffee Brownies (page 172)

1 cup cold brewed double-strength coffee, divided

1 package (8 ounces) cream cheese, softened

1 cup cold milk

1 package (4-serving size) chocolate flavor instant pudding and pie filling

1 tub (8 ounces) frozen whipped topping, thawed, divided

½ pint raspberries

Additional raspberries, for garnish (optional)

✦ **PREPARE** the Coffee Brownies.

✦ **CUT** the brownies into ½-inch squares. Sprinkle with ¼ cup of the coffee.

✦ **BEAT** the cream cheese and the remaining ¾ cup of coffee in a large bowl with a wire whisk until smooth. Gradually beat in the cold milk until smooth. Add the pudding mix. Beat with the wire whisk for 1 minute. Gently stir in 2 cups of the whipped topping.

✦ **LAYER** half of the brownies, half of the raspberries, and half of the pudding mixture in a large glass bowl; repeat the layers.

✦ **REFRIGERATE** for 1 hour or until ready to serve. Top with the remaining whipped topping and additional raspberries, if desired.

Makes 8 servings

COFFEE HOUSE INSPIRATION

For toffee lovers, chop 3 chocolate-covered toffee bars and include in the layers. Chop an additional chocolate-covered toffee bar for garnish, if desired.

awesome
sundae pie

After a night at the movies, invite your guests to help you decorate the dessert.

Or let each person create their own "sundae" pie.

Prep: 20 minutes • Refrigerate: 3 hours

2 tablespoons instant coffee

1 tablespoon butter *or* margarine, melted

6 squares (6 ounces) semi-sweet chocolate

¾ cup toasted sweetened flaked coconut

¾ cup finely chopped toasted nuts

4 cups Coffee Ice Cream (page 195)

Whipped cream, chopped nuts, and maraschino cherries, for garnish (optional)

Mexican Chocolate Sauce (page 195)

✦ **LINE** a 9-inch pie plate with foil; lightly butter the foil.

✦ **STIR** the instant coffee and butter in a large microwavable bowl until well blended. Add the chocolate. Microwave on High for 2 minutes, or until the chocolate is almost melted. Stir until the chocolate is completely melted. Stir in the coconut and nuts. Spread the mixture evenly on the bottom and up the sides of the prepared pie plate.

✦ **REFRIGERATE** for 1 hour or until the crust is firm. Lift the crust out of the pie plate. Carefully peel away the foil. Return the crust to the pie plate or place it on a serving plate. Fill the crust with scoops of Coffee Ice Cream and cover.

✦ **FREEZE** for 2 hours or until firm. Let stand at room temperature for 10 minutes or until the pie can be cut easily. Garnish with whipped cream, nuts, and maraschino cherries, if desired. Cut into slices to serve. Serve with Mexican Chocolate Sauce, if desired. Store the leftover pie in the freezer.

Makes 8 servings.

COFFEE HOUSE TIP

In place of the homemade *coffee ice cream* in this recipe, you can substitute your favorite flavors of store-bought ice cream.

awesome sundae pie

chocolate lover's
cheesecake

*Chocolate lovers will swoon when you bring out this luscious cheesecake.
Decorate the edge of the cheesecake with a ring of white or dark chocolate
curls to make it look extra special.*

Prep: 10 minutes • Bake: 40 minutes • Refrigerate: 3 hours

4 squares (4 ounces) semi-sweet chocolate,
   melted, slightly cooled

2 tablespoons instant coffee

2 packages (8 ounces each) cream cheese,
   softened

½ cup granulated sugar

½ teaspoon vanilla extract

2 large eggs

1 prepared chocolate flavor crumb crust
   (6 ounces *or* 9 inches)

✦ **HEAT** the oven to 350°F.

✦ **STIR** the melted chocolate and instant coffee in a
small bowl until well blended; set aside.

✦ **BEAT** the cream cheese, sugar, and vanilla in a
large bowl with an electric mixer set on medium
speed until well blended. Beat in the eggs until
blended. Stir in the melted chocolate mixture. Pour
the mixture into the crust.

✦ **BAKE** for 40 minutes or until the center is almost
set. Cool completely on a wire rack.

✦ **REFRIGERATE** for at least 3 hours or overnight.
Cut into slices. Store the leftover cheesecake in the
refrigerator.

Makes 8 servings

COFFEE HOUSE TIP

**You can soften cream cheese quickly in the
microwave. Place 1 completely unwrapped
package of cream cheese in a microwavable
bowl. Microwave on High for 15 seconds.
Add 15 seconds for each additional
package of cream cheese.**

tiramisu

Tiramisu literally translates to "pick-me-up" in Italian, which is exactly how your guests will feel when they sample this sublime creation.

Prep: 20 minutes • Refrigerate: 3 hours

½ cup cooled freshly brewed double-strength coffee

⅓ cup granulated sugar, divided

2 tablespoons Marsala wine

2 teaspoons vanilla extract, divided

24 hard ladyfingers

1 pound mascarpone cheese (see Coffee House Inspiration)

1½ cups heavy (whipping) cream, whipped

2 teaspoons unsweetened cocoa powder *or* grated semi-sweet chocolate

+ **MIX** the coffee, 2 tablespoons of the sugar, the wine, and 1 teaspoon of the vanilla in a small bowl; set aside.

+ **ARRANGE** half of the ladyfingers in the bottom of a 9-inch-square dish. Brush the ladyfingers with half of the coffee mixture, allowing time for them to absorb the coffee mixture.

+ **STIR** the mascarpone cheese, and the remaining sugar and vanilla until well blended. (Do not beat.) Gently fold in the whipped cream. Spoon half of the cheese mixture over the ladyfingers. Brush the remaining ladyfingers with the remaining coffee mixture. Place on top of the cheese mixture in the dish.

+ **SPREAD** the remaining cheese mixture over the ladyfingers. Sift the cocoa powder over the cheese mixture or sprinkle with the grated chocolate.

+ **REFRIGERATE** for 3 hours or until ready to serve. Cut into squares to serve.

Makes 8 servings

COFFEE HOUSE TIP

Mascarpone cheese is a rich creamy Italian cheese that is available in Italian food stores and specialty food stores.

coffee caramel
nut tart

When this dessert is cut, the nuts form an almost mosaic-like pattern.

Prep: 30 minutes • Bake: 10 minutes

1 ½ cups graham cracker crumbs

⅓ cup butter *or* margarine, melted

¼ cup firmly packed brown sugar

¼ teaspoon ground cinnamon

½ cup heavy (whipping) cream

2 tablespoons instant coffee

1 package (14 ounces) caramels, unwrapped

4 cups toasted pecans *or* almonds

Melted semi-sweet chocolate for drizzling
    on the dessert *or* plate (optional)

✦ **HEAT** the oven to 325°F.

✦ **MIX** the crumbs, butter, brown sugar, and cinnamon in a medium bowl until well mixed. Press the mixture onto the bottom and 1 inch up the sides of a 9-inch springform pan. Bake for 10 minutes or until lightly browned. Cool on a wire rack.

✦ **STIR** the cream and instant coffee in a large microwavable bowl until well blended. Add the caramels. Microwave on High for 2 to 3 minutes, stirring every minute. Stir until the caramels are completely melted. Stir in the nuts. Spoon the mixture into the baked crust. Spread the top evenly with a knife.

✦ **REFRIGERATE** for about 1 hour or until firm. Cut into slices to serve. Drizzle the tart and/or plate with the melted chocolate, if desired.

Makes 10 to 12 servings

COFFEE HOUSE INSPIRATIONS

Substitute 4 cups of mixed nuts for the pecans to create an especially sophisticated nut pie.

Drizzling desserts or dessert plates with thin lines of melted chocolate can help you present your desserts like a pro. See our easy technique on page 20.

coffee caramel nut tart

coffee brownies

Great for snacking! Small chunks of these brownies also play an important part in Mocha Passion (page 165).

Prep: 10 minutes • Bake: 30 minutes

4 large eggs

2 tablespoons instant coffee

1 teaspoon vanilla extract

¾ cup (1½ sticks) butter *or* margarine

4 squares (4 ounces) unsweetened chocolate

2 cups granulated sugar

1 cup all-purpose flour

1 cup toasted coarsely chopped nuts (optional)

Bittersweet Coffee Glaze (optional), (page 176)

✦ **HEAT** the oven to 350°F. Line a 13x9-inch baking pan with foil; lightly butter the foil.

✦ **STIR** the eggs, instant coffee, and vanilla in a small bowl until well blended; set aside.

✦ **MICROWAVE** the butter and chocolate in a microwavable bowl on High for 2 minutes or until the butter is melted. Stir until the chocolate is completely melted.

✦ **STIR** the sugar into the chocolate mixture until well blended. Mix in the egg mixture. Stir in the flour and nuts. Spread the batter in the prepared pan.

✦ **BAKE** for 30 minutes or until a toothpick inserted in the center comes out with fudgy crumbs. (Do not overbake.) Cool completely in the pan on a wire rack. Spread the Bittersweet Coffee Glaze over the brownies, if desired. Cut into squares to serve. Store in a tightly covered container.

Makes 24 brownies

COFFEE HOUSE TIP

In most cases, it is easier to neatly cut bar-shaped brownies, bars, and other desserts if you line the pan with foil first. For a 13x9-inch pan, line the pan so that the foil extends 2 inches beyond the two long sides of the pan. If indicated in the recipe, lightly butter the bottom and sides of the foil-lined pan. After baking (or in some cases, refrigerating or freezing), use the two ends of the foil as handles and lift the dessert out of the pan onto a cutting board. Cut into rectangles or squares. Use this same technique to line 8- and 9-inch square pans and loaf pans.

easy mocha fondue

Here's a dessert that gets everyone involved as they take the plunge and dip their fruit, cookies, or pretzels into this coffee-enhanced chocolate fondue.

Prep: 5 minutes• Microwave: 1½ minutes

½ cup heavy (whipping) cream

2 tablespoons instant coffee

⅔ cup light corn syrup

8 squares (8 ounces) semi-sweet chocolate, coarsely chopped

Assorted fresh fruit, dried fruit, cookies, and pretzels to use as dippers

✦ **STIR** the heavy cream and instant coffee in a large microwavable bowl until well blended. Stir in the corn syrup.

✦ **MICROWAVE** on High for 1½ minutes or until the mixture comes to a boil. Add the chocolate and stir until completely melted. Serve warm as a dip with the fresh and/or dried fruit, cookies, and pretzels.

Makes about 1½ cups

café caramel fondue

All dessert fondues do not have to be chocolate. Next time, enjoy this coffee-caramel version with your guests or serve both of these fondues.

Prep: 10 minutes • Microwave: 5 minutes

1 bag (14 ounces) caramels, unwrapped

¼ cup brewed double-strength coffee

¼ cup milk

Assorted fresh fruit, cake cubes, and cookies to use as dippers.

✦ **MICROWAVE** the caramels, coffee, and milk in a large microwavable bowl on High for 3½ to 5 minutes or until the caramels are melted and the mixture is smooth, stirring every 2 minutes. Serve warm as a dip with the fruit, cake cubes, and cookies.

Makes about 1⅓ cups

petite mocha cakes

These individual desserts are made to be served warm. The outside cake surrounds a molten chocolate filling, providing a delightful contrast of textures.

Prep: 15 minutes • Bake: 12 minutes

¼ cup granulated sugar

¾ cup butter, cut into pieces

6 squares (6 ounces) bittersweet chocolate

2 tablespoons instant coffee

4 large eggs

⅔ cup powdered sugar

1 teaspoon vanilla extract

⅓ cup all-purpose flour

¼ teaspoon ground cinnamon

Whipped cream

Powdered sugar, raspberries, and fresh mint sprigs, for garnish (optional)

Piped Chocolate Shapes, for garnish (optional)

✦ **HEAT** the oven to 400°F. Using no-stick cooking spray, lightly spray six (4-ounce) custard cups or ramekins. Dust with the granulated sugar.

✦ **MICROWAVE** the butter, chocolate, and instant coffee in a large microwavable bowl on High for 1 minute or until the butter has melted. Stir until the chocolate is completely melted. Freeze for 5 minutes or until cool, stirring occasionally.

✦ **BEAT** the eggs, powdered sugar, and vanilla in a large bowl with an electric mixer set on high speed for 2 to 3 minutes. Beat in the cooled chocolate mixture. Mix the flour and cinnamon in a small bowl. Beat into the chocolate mixture until just blended, scraping the side of the bowl. Divide the batter evenly among the prepared cups. Place the cups 2 inches apart on a large baking sheet.

✦ **BAKE** for 10 to 12 minutes or until the cakes are lightly puffed and feel firm at the edges and soft in the center when pressed with a fingertip. Cool the cakes in the dishes for 5 minutes, then invert onto individual serving plates. Serve warm with whipped cream. Sprinkle with powdered sugar and garnish with raspberries and mint sprigs, if desired. Garnish each cake with a Piped Chocolate Shape, if desired.

Makes 6 servings

COFFEE HOUSE INSPIRATION

These *petite mocha cakes* are garnished with *piped chocolate coffee cup shapes*. See page 160 for directions.

petite mocha cake

easy truffles

Place each of these truffles in an individual paper candy cup and display them on an elegant cake stand as a welcome after dinner nibble.

Prep: 5 minutes • Microwave: 2 minutes • Refrigerate: 1½ hours

6 tablespoons heavy (whipping) cream

2 teaspoons instant coffee

6 squares (6 ounces) white chocolate, chopped

2 squares (2 ounces) semi-sweet chocolate, chopped

Cocoa powder, sweetened flaked coconut, cookie crumbs, *or* chopped nuts to coat the truffles

✦ **STIR** the cream and instant coffee in a large microwavable bowl until well blended. Add the chocolates. Microwave on High for 2 minutes, stirring halfway through cooking time. Stir until the chocolates are completely melted and the mixture is smooth.

✦ **REFRIGERATE** for about 1 to 1½ hours or until firm enough to handle. Shape into 1-inch balls. Roll in cocoa, coconut flakes, cookie crumbs, or nuts. Store the truffles in the refrigerator.

Makes about 2 dozen truffles

bittersweet coffee glaze

This glaze is wonderful on the Coffee Brownies (page 172).

Prep: 5 minutes • Microwave: 2 minutes

6 squares (6 ounces) bittersweet chocolate

5 tablespoons corn syrup

1 tablespoon butter *or* margarine

1 teaspoon instant coffee

✦ **MICROWAVE** the chocolate, corn syrup, butter, and instant coffee in a medium microwavable bowl on High for 2 minutes or until the butter is melted Stir until the chocolate is melted. Cool slightly. Spread over the brownies, cakes, and cookies.

Makes about 1 cup

chocolate mousse
coffee

A fluffy "chocolate mousse" mixture makes a regular cup of java taste special.

Prep: 10 minutes

3 squares (3 ounces) unsweetened chocolate
½ cup freshly brewed coffee
¾ cup granulated sugar
½ cup heavy (whipping) cream, whipped
Hot freshly brewed coffee, for serving

PREPARE THE "CHOCOLATE MOUSSE":

✦ **PLACE** the chocolate and the ½ cup of coffee in a heavy saucepan on very low heat. Stir constantly with a wire whisk until the chocolate is melted and smooth. Stir in the sugar. Bring the mixture to a boil. Reduce the heat to low and simmer for 4 minutes, stirring constantly. Pour into a large bowl. Cool to room temperature. Gently stir the whipped cream into the cooled chocolate mixture. Store the "chocolate mousse," covered, in the refrigerator.

Makes about 1⅔ cups "chocolate mousse" mixture or enough for 24 servings

TO SERVE:

✦ **PLACE** 1 rounded tablespoon of the "chocolate mousse" in a cup or mug. Stir in ¾ cup of hot coffee until well blended. Serve immediately.

Makes 1 serving

cappuccino cookie roll

Cappuccino mix adds an updated flavor twist to this all-time favorite classic dessert.

Prep: 15 minutes • Refrigerate: 4 hours

1 envelope instant cappuccino mix, any flavor

2 tablespoons hot water

1 tub (8 ounces) frozen whipped topping, thawed

1 package (9 ounces) chocolate wafer cookies

Chocolate-covered coffee beans *or* chocolate curls, for garnish (optional)

✦ **STIR** the cappuccino mix and hot water in a large bowl until well blended. Cool. Gently stir in the whipped topping until blended. Spread ½ tablespoon of the mixture on each cookie. Begin stacking the cookies together and stand them on edge on a serving platter to make a 14-inch log. Frost with the remaining whipped topping mixture.

✦ **REFRIGERATE** for 4 hours or until ready to serve. Garnish with chocolate-covered coffee beans or chocolate curls, if desired. Slice the roll at an angle to serve.

Makes 12 servings

vanilla coffee

A touch of vanilla and brown sugar turns a cup of coffee into a delicious treat.

Prep: 5 minutes

½ cup ground coffee

¼ cup firmly packed brown sugar

1 to 2 tablespoons vanilla extract

6 cups cold water

✦ **PLACE** the coffee in the filter in the brew basket of a coffee maker. Place the sugar in the empty pot of the coffee maker.

✦ **PREPARE** the coffee with the cold water. When the brewing is complete, stir in the vanilla until well mixed. Pour into large cups or mugs.

Makes 6 servings.

COFFEE HOUSE INSPIRATION

For a Cinnamon Variation: Add ¼ teaspoon ground cinnamon to the coffee in the filter before brewing.

cappuccino cookie roll

toffee coffee

Caramel and chocolate dessert toppings flavor this sweetly delicious coffee.
For extra pizzazz, serve it with whipped cream and a sprinkling
of chopped chocolate-covered toffee.

Prep: 5 minutes

6 tablespoons ground coffee

⅓ cup each caramel and chocolate dessert
   toppings

4 ½ cups cold water

Whipped cream and chopped chocolate-
   covered toffee bars, for garnish
   (optional)

◆ **PLACE** the coffee in the filter in the brew basket
of a coffee maker. Place the caramel and chocolate
toppings in the empty pot of a coffee maker.

◆ **PREPARE** the coffee with the cold water. When
the brewing is complete, stir until well mixed. Pour
into large cups or mugs. Top each serving with
whipped cream and chopped chocolate-covered
toffee bars, if desired. Serve immediately.

Makes 6 servings

COFFEE HOUSE INSPIRATION

**For a Cool Variation: Prepare the coffee as
directed and refrigerate for a cold beverage.
Serve over ice.**

A DROP OF HISTORY

1907   While on a visit to "The Hermitage," former President Andrew Jackson's home in
Nashville, Tennessee, President Theodore Roosevelt is served a cup of Maxwell House
coffee. According to legend, he comments that it is "good to the last drop."

tropical frappé

Cappuccino mix and pineapple combine to make this delightful beverage.

Prep: 5 minutes

1 envelope instant cappuccino mix, any flavor
½ cup cold milk
1 can (8 ounces) crushed pineapple in juice, undrained
1 small ripe banana
1 pint (2 cups) vanilla ice cream, softened
Whipped cream and toasted coconut (optional)

✦ **PLACE** all of the ingredients in a blender container; cover. Blend on high speed until smooth. Pour into tall glasses. Top with whipped cream and toasted coconut, if desired. Serve immediately.

Makes 4 servings

chocolate cherry coffee

Maraschino cherry juice and chocolate syrup make this a distinctive dessert coffee.

¼ cup ground coffee
¼ cup chocolate syrup
¼ cup maraschino cherry juice
2½ cups cold water
Whipped cream, chopped chocolate, and maraschino cherries, for garnish (optional)

✦ **PLACE** the coffee in the filter in the brew basket of a coffee maker. Pour the chocolate syrup and cherry juice into the empty pot of the coffee maker.

✦ **PREPARE** the coffee with the cold water. When the brewing is complete, stir until well mixed. Pour into large cups or mugs. Top each serving with whipped cream, chopped chocolate, and a maraschino cherry, if desired. Serve immediately.

Makes 4 servings

midnight snack

Late at night, there is nothing quite like

chocolate toffee bars (page 190) to lull you into

a restful sleep. Unless, of course, you would prefer a bowl of

homemade *coffee ice cream* blanketed in

mexican chocolate sauce (page 195).

A *chunksicle* (page 192),

on the other hand, can be carried INTO bed—

or maybe you would prefer a slice of

midnight bliss cake (page 200).

With so many choices, it may be comforting to realize

that the hours are already ticking away to breakfast time,

when you can again look forward to that

shake awake smoothie (page 26)!

toffee bar dessert
marbled mocha bars
coffee cup triangles
mocha brownies
almond cappuccino ice cream
chocolate toffee bars
chunksicles
frozen coffee pie
coffee ice cream
mexican chocolate sauce
mocha cereal squares
fudge balls
cappuccino spice dessert
hot coffee float
frozen "hot chocolate" coffee
midnight bliss cake
ice cream "tiramisu"
candy bar shake
cappuccino peanut butter snack mix
mocha mania cookies
java mini cakes
java pudding frosting
black & white chocolate coffee
double capped cappuccino

toffee bar dessert

Toffee bits and nuts form the crust of this layered refrigerated dessert.

Prep: 20 minutes • Bake: 10 minutes • Refrigerate: 3 hours

1 cup all-purpose flour

½ cup finely chopped toasted pecans

1 cup toffee bits, divided

¼ cup granulated sugar

½ cup (1 stick) butter *or* margarine, melted

1 cup cold brewed double-strength coffee

1 cup cold milk

2 packages (4-serving size each) butterscotch flavor instant pudding and pie filling

1 tub (8 ounces) frozen whipped topping, thawed, divided

+ **HEAT** the oven to 400°F. Line a 13x9-inch baking pan with foil; lightly butter the foil.

+ **MIX** the flour, pecans, ½ cup of the toffee bits, sugar, and butter in a large bowl until well mixed. Press the mixture firmly onto the bottom of the prepared pan. Bake for 10 minutes or until lightly browned. Cool on a wire rack.

+ **POUR** the cold coffee and milk into a large bowl. Add the pudding mixes. Beat with a wire whisk for 1 minute. Spread 1½ cups of the pudding on the bottom of the crust. Gently stir half of the whipped topping into the remaining pudding. Spread over the pudding in the pan. Top with the remaining whipped topping. Sprinkle with the remaining toffee bits.

+ **REFRIGERATE** for 3 hours or until ready to serve. Cut into squares to serve.

Makes 15 servings

COFFEE HOUSE TIP

Toast nuts *before* finely chopping them. To toast nuts, spread them in a shallow pan. Toast at 400°F for 8 to 10 minutes or until the nuts are golden, stirring them frequently.

Not only are toasted nuts great in baked goods, they are also superb when sprinkled on top of ice cream or other desserts.

marbled
mocha bars

Semi-sweet and white chocolates are swirled together to create an easy frosting for these moist bars. Walnuts add crunch to both the cookie base and the topping.

Prep: 15 minutes • Bake: 25 minutes

COOKIE BASE:

1 large egg

2 tablespoons instant coffee

½ cup (1 stick) butter *or* margarine, softened

¾ cup firmly packed brown sugar

1 cup all-purpose flour

½ teaspoon baking soda

¼ teaspoon salt

4 squares (4 ounces) semi-sweet chocolate, chopped

3 squares (3 ounces) white chocolate, chopped

½ cup chopped walnuts

TOPPING:

4 squares (4 ounces) semi-sweet chocolate, chopped

3 squares (3 ounces) white chocolate, chopped

½ cup chopped walnuts

PREPARE THE COOKIE BASE:

✦ **HEAT** the oven to 350°F. Line a 9-inch square baking pan with foil; lightly butter the foil.

✦ **STIR** the egg and instant coffee in a small bowl until well blended; set aside.

✦ **BEAT** the butter, brown sugar, and egg mixture in a large bowl with an electric mixer set on medium speed until light and fluffy. Mix in the flour, baking soda, and salt. Stir in the chopped chocolates and walnuts. Spread the batter in the prepared pan.

✦ **BAKE** for 25 minutes or until a toothpick inserted in the center comes out almost clean. (Do not overbake.) Set the pan on a wire rack.

PREPARE THE TOPPING:

✦ **SPRINKLE** the surface of the cookie base with the chopped chocolates. Cover the pan with foil. Let stand for 5 minutes or until the chocolates are melted. Swirl the chocolates with a small knife to marbleize. Sprinkle with the walnuts. Cool in the pan on the wire rack until the chocolate is firm. Cut into bars to serve. Store in a tightly covered container.

Makes 3 dozen bars

coffee cup triangles

*A moist fudgy brownie is blanketed with a coffee-cream cheese
mixture to create this rich two-layer dessert.*

Prep: 15 minutes • Bake: 45 minutes

BROWNIE BOTTOM:

4 large eggs

2 tablespoons instant coffee

¾ cup (1½ sticks) butter *or* margarine

4 squares (4 ounces) unsweetened chocolate

2 cups granulated sugar

1 cup all-purpose flour

CHEESECAKE TOPPING:

3 large eggs

2 tablespoons instant coffee

3 packages (8 ounces each) cream cheese, softened

¾ cup granulated sugar

1 teaspoon vanilla extract

½ cup sour cream

Piped Chocolate Coffee Cup Shapes (optional),
    for garnish (page 160)

PREPARE THE BROWNIE BOTTOM:

✦ **HEAT** the oven to 350°F. Line a 13x9-inch baking
pan with foil; lightly butter the foil.

✦ **STIR** the eggs and instant coffee in a small bowl
until well blended; set aside.

✦ **MICROWAVE** the butter and chocolate in a large
microwavable bowl on High for 2 minutes or until
the butter has melted. Stir until the chocolate is
completely melted.

coffee cup triangle

✦ **STIR** the sugar into the chocolate mixture until well
blended. Mix in the egg mixture. Stir in the flour until
well blended. Spread the batter in the prepared pan.

PREPARE THE CHEESECAKE TOPPING:

✦ **STIR** the eggs and instant coffee in a small bowl
until well blended; set aside.

✦ **BEAT** the cream cheese, sugar, and vanilla in a
large bowl with an electric mixer set on high speed
until well blended. Add the egg mixture and mix on
low speed until blended. Beat in the sour cream.
Spoon the mixture evenly over the brownie bottom.

✦ **BAKE** for 40 to 45 minutes or until the center is
almost set. Run a knife or a metal spatula around the
edges of the pan to loosen the brownies from the sides.
Cool completely on a wire rack.

✦ **REFRIGERATE** for 4 hours or overnight. Cut into
triangles or squares. Garnish with the Piped
Chocolate Coffee Cup Shapes, if desired. Store the
leftover triangles in the refrigerator.

Makes 24 servings

COFFEE HOUSE INSPIRATIONS

These cheesecake triangles are garnished
with *piped chocolate coffee cup shapes* (see
page 160 for directions), but simple chocolate curls or chocolate-covered coffee beans
would also look pretty.

mocha brownies

These dense, fudgy brownies were carefully created to satisfy the most discerning of chocolate aficionados.

Prep: 15 minutes • Bake: 40 minutes

8 squares (8 ounces) semi-sweet chocolate *or*
   6 squares (6 ounces) bittersweet chocolate,
   divided
¼ cup (½ stick) butter *or* margarine
¾ cup granulated sugar, divided
4 tablespoons instant coffee, divided
3 large eggs, divided
¾ cup all-purpose flour
⅔ cup heavy (whipping) cream

✦ **HEAT** the oven to 350°F. Line an 8-inch square baking pan with foil; lightly butter the foil.

✦ **MICROWAVE** 2 squares of the chocolate and the butter in a medium microwavable bowl on High for 1 ½ minutes or until the butter has melted. Stir until the chocolate is completely melted. Stir in ½ cup of the sugar and 2 tablespoons of the instant coffee. Stir in 1 egg until well blended. Stir in the flour. Spread the batter in the prepared pan.

✦ **MICROWAVE** the remaining chocolate (6 squares if using semi-sweet *or* 4 squares if using bittersweet), the cream, and the remaining 2 tablespoons of instant coffee in a microwavable bowl on High for 1½ minutes. Stir until the chocolate is melted.

✦ **BEAT** the remaining 2 eggs and remaining ¼ cup sugar in a small bowl with an electric mixer set on high speed for 1 minute or until thick and lemon-colored. Beat in the chocolate mixture. Pour the mixture over the batter in the pan.

✦ **BAKE** for 35 to 40 minutes or until the truffle topping is set and the edges begin to pull away from the sides of the pan. Cool completely in the pan on a wire rack. Cut into squares to serve. Store in a tightly covered container.

Makes 16 brownies

almond cappuccino
ice cream

Ice cream is ideal for satisfying late-night cravings.
This easy almond-flavored recipe is ideal to have on hand.

Prep: 10 minutes • Freeze: 4 hours

1 can (14 ounces) fat free sweetened
    condensed milk
½ cup cold milk
2 envelopes instant cappuccino mix, any flavor
2 cups heavy (whipping) cream
1 cup toasted sliced almonds

✦ **STIR** the condensed milk, cold milk, and cappuccino mix in a medium bowl until well blended.

✦ **BEAT** the cream in a chilled large bowl with an
electric mixer set on medium speed until soft peaks
form. (Do not overbeat.) Gently stir in the cappuccino mixture and the almonds. Pour the mixture
into a 1½-quart metal bowl. Cover.

✦ **FREEZE** for 4 hours or until firm, stirring once
after 2 hours or when the edges begin to harden.
Store the ice cream in a tightly covered container
in the freezer for up to 1 week.

Makes about 12 servings

COFFEE HOUSE INSPIRATION

**Dress up beverages or desserts with a quick
and easy cappuccino-flavored topping.
Dissolve one envelope of instant cappuccino
mix, any flavor, in 2 tablespoons of hot water
in a large bowl; cool. Gently stir in 1 tub
(8 ounces) thawed frozen whipped topping
until blended. Store in the refrigerator until
ready to serve. Use as a topping for fruit,
cake, ice cream, or pudding. Or serve with
hot or cold beverages. (See the recipe for
double capped cappuccino on page 206.)**

chocolate
toffee bars

Coffee gives the classic flavor combination of chocolate and toffee an unusual accent. For another change of pace, cut these layered cookies into triangles instead of rectangles.

Prep: 15 minutes • Bake: 40 minutes

CRUST:

¾ cup butter *or* margarine, softened

¾ cup firmly packed brown sugar

1 large egg yolk

1½ cups all-purpose flour

¼ teaspoon salt

COFFEE TOPPING:

1 tablespoon instant coffee

2 teaspoons vanilla extract

1 can (14 ounces) sweetened condensed milk

2 tablespoons butter *or* margarine

6 squares (6 ounces) semi-sweet chocolate, chopped

6 squares (6 ounces) white chocolate, chopped

1 cup toasted chopped pecans

PREPARE THE CRUST:

✦ **HEAT** the oven to 350°F. Line a 13x9-inch baking pan with foil; lightly butter the foil.

✦ **BEAT** the butter and the brown sugar in a large bowl with an electric mixer set on medium speed until smooth. Add the egg yolk and beat well. Stir in the flour and salt until well mixed. Press the mixture into the bottom of the prepared pan.

✦ **BAKE** for 20 minutes or until golden brown. Set the pan on a wire rack to cool slightly.

PREPARE THE TOPPING:

✦ **STIR** the instant coffee and vanilla in a large microwavable bowl until well blended. Stir in the condensed milk and butter until well blended.

✦ **MICROWAVE** on High for 4 minutes, stirring every minute or until the mixture is thick and smooth. Spread evenly over the baked layer in the pan.

✦ **BAKE** for 12 to 15 minutes or until set. Sprinkle the surface with the chopped chocolates in a decorative pattern. Bake for 1 to 2 minutes longer or until the chocolates are melted. Use a spatula to smooth the surface evenly. Sprinkle with the pecans. Cool completely on the wire rack. Refrigerate 30 minutes or until the chocolate is firm. Cut into bars or diamond shapes to serve. Store in a tightly covered container.

Makes about 3 dozen bars

chocolate toffee bars

chunksicles

These jumbo frozen bars would be a welcome sight when you open up the freezer "at the midnight hour." Packed generously with chunks of dark and white chocolate, they are cleverly made using empty juice drink boxes as molds.

Prep: 15 minutes • Freeze: 6 hours

5 (8.45-ounce) empty juice drink boxes

1½ cups cold half-and-half *or* milk

1 package (4-serving size) vanilla flavor instant pudding and pie filling

1 envelope instant cappuccino mix, any flavor

1 tub (8 ounces) frozen whipped topping, thawed

2 squares (2 ounces) semi-sweet chocolate, chopped

2 squares (2 ounces) white chocolate, chopped

1 cup toasted slivered almonds

5 wooden Popsicle sticks

♦ **EMPTY** and rinse the juice drink boxes. Cut 1 inch off the top of each box.

♦ **POUR** the cold half-and-half into a large bowl. Add the pudding and cappuccino mixes. Beat with a wire whisk for 1 minute. Gently stir in the whipped topping. Stir in the chocolate chunks and almonds. Spoon the mixture evenly into the prepared boxes. Insert a wooden stick into each box.

♦ **FREEZE** for 6 hours or overnight until firm. To serve, dip each *chunksicle* in hot water for 10 seconds. Carefully slide the juice box off and set the *chunksicle* back into the freezer to firm up the outside. Wrap leftover *chunksicles* in plastic wrap and store in the freezer.

Makes 5 chunksicles

COFFEE HOUSE INSPIRATION

Drizzle the frozen *chunksicles* with melted chocolate for extra indulgence. See our easy technique on page 20. After drizzling with the chocolate, place the *chunksicles* back in the freezer for a few minutes until the chocolate is firm.

frozen coffee pie

After the party is over, a wedge of this pie could be just what you are looking for.

Prep: 15 minutes • Freeze: 6 hours

¾ cup cold brewed strong coffee

¾ cup cold half-and-half *or* milk

1 package (4-serving size) vanilla flavor instant pudding and pie filling

1 tub (8 ounces) frozen whipped topping, thawed

1 prepared chocolate flavor crumb crust (6 ounces *or* 9 inches)

✦ **POUR** the cold coffee and half-and-half into a large bowl. Add the pudding mix. Beat with a wire whisk for 1 minute. Let stand for 5 minutes or until the mixture thickens. Gently stir in the whipped topping. Spoon the mixture into the crust.

✦ **FREEZE** for 6 hours or overnight until firm. Let stand at room temperature for about 10 minutes or until the pie can be cut easily. Cut into slices to serve. Store the leftover pie in the freezer.

Makes 8 servings

marvelous mix-ins

For delightful variations, stir one of the following into the filling mixture before spooning it into the crust:

½ cup coarsely chopped chocolate-covered coffee beans

1½ cups coarsely chopped biscotti

½ cup each semi-sweet chocolate chips, miniature marshmallows, and chopped nuts

1½ cups chopped chocolate sandwich cookies

1 cup chopped chocolate-covered toffee bars

COFFEE HOUSE INSPIRATIONS

Substitute 1 tablespoon of instant coffee for the brewed coffee and increase the half-and-half to 1½ cups.

Spread ½ cup of fudge sauce on the bottom of the crust before filling. Serve the pie with additional fudge sauce, if desired.

coffee ice cream

Homemade coffee ice cream makes a marvelous bedtime snack.

Prep: 15 minutes • Refrigerate: 1 hour • Freeze: 2 hours

1 cup cold brewed double-strength coffee
1 cup heavy (whipping) cream
1 can (14 ounces) sweetened condensed milk

✦ **STIR** the cold coffee, cream, and condensed milk in a large bowl until well blended. Refrigerate for about 1 hour to chill.

✦ **FREEZE** the coffee mixture in an ice cream maker according to the manufacturer's directions. Spoon the ice cream into a 1-quart freezer container and cover. Freeze for about 2 hours or until firm.

Makes about 1 quart

COFFEE HOUSE INSPIRATIONS

Try making this with some of our mix-in suggestions. Prepare the *coffee ice cream* as directed, stirring in 1 cup of any of the following as the ice cream begins to freeze in the ice cream maker: coarsely chopped chocolate-covered coffee beans; amaretti cookies, broken into pieces; coarsely chopped chocolate-covered toffee bars; *or* coarsely chopped biscotti.

mexican chocolate sauce

Cinnamon and coffee add intriguing layers of flavor to this rich chocolate sauce.

Prep: 5 minutes • Microwave: 4 ½ minutes

2 squares (2 ounces) unsweetened chocolate
⅓ cup brewed double strength coffee
½ cup granulated sugar
3 tablespoons butter or margarine
¼ teaspoon ground cinnamon
¼ teaspoon vanilla extract

✦ **MICROWAVE** the chocolate and coffee in a large microwavable bowl on High for 1½ minutes, stirring halfway through the cooking time. Stir until the chocolate is completely melted. Stir in the sugar.

✦ **MICROWAVE** on High for 3 minutes, stirring after each minute. Stir in the butter, cinnamon, and vanilla until the butter has completely melted. Serve warm. Store the leftover sauce in the refrigerator.

Makes about 1 cup sauce

coffee ice cream with mexican chocolate sauce

mocha cereal squares

These chewy bars are a great companion to the late-late-show.

Prep: 5 minutes • Microwave: 2 minutes

1 tablespoon instant coffee

1 teaspoon hot water

¼ cup (½ stick) butter *or* margarine

1 package (10½ ounces) miniature
   marshmallows (6 cups)

1 package (13 ounces) cocoa flavor crisp rice
   cereal (about 8½ cups)

✦ **LINE** a 13x9-inch baking pan with foil; lightly
butter the foil.

✦ **STIR** the instant coffee and water in a small bowl
until well blended; set aside.

✦ **MICROWAVE** the butter in a large microwavable
bowl on High for 45 seconds or until it has melted.
Add the marshmallows and the coffee mixture and
stir to coat evenly. Microwave 1½ minutes longer
or until the marshmallows are melted and smooth,
stirring after 45 seconds. Add the cereal and mix to
coat well. Press the mixture firmly into the prepared pan. Cool. Cut into squares to serve.

Makes about 2 dozen squares

fudge balls

Keep these in your refrigerator to satisfy your chocolate cravings any time of night or day.

Prep: 10 minutes • Microwave: 2 minutes

8 squares (8 ounces) semi-sweet chocolate

⅓ cup sweetened condensed milk

¼ cup brewed double strength coffee

½ cup chopped nuts

1 teaspoon vanilla extract

✦ **LINE** an 8-inch square pan with foil; set aside.

✦ **MICROWAVE** the chocolate, condensed milk
and coffee in a large microwavable bowl on High

for 2 minutes or until the chocolate is almost
melted, stirring halfway through the heating time.
Stir until the chocolate is completely melted. Stir in
the nuts and vanilla. Spread into the prepared pan.

✦ **REFRIGERATE** for 2 hours or until the mixture is
firm enough to handle. Shape into 1-inch balls.
Roll in coatings, if desired (see Coffee House
Inspiration on page 197). Store in a tightly covered
container in the refrigerator.

Makes about 2 dozen fudge balls

cappuccino spice dessert

This dessert is elegantly flavored with cappuccino and a hint of cinnamon.

Prep: 15 minutes • Refrigerate: 1 hour

1 cup cold half-and-half *or* milk

1 package (4-serving size) vanilla flavor instant
    pudding and pie filling

1 envelope instant cappuccino mix, any flavor

1 tub (8 ounces) frozen whipped topping,
    thawed, divided

⅛ teaspoon ground cinnamon

Additional ground cinnamon, for sprinkling
    on desserts (optional)

♦ **POUR** the cold milk into a medium bowl. Add the pudding and cappuccino mixes. Beat with a wire whisk for 1 minute. Gently stir in 2 cups of the whipped topping. Spoon the mixture into 6 dessert dishes.

♦ **REFRIGERATE** for 1 hour or until ready to serve. Just before serving, gently stir the remaining whipped topping and cinnamon in a small bowl until blended. Spread the whipped topping mixture over the pudding mixture in the dishes. Sprinkle with additional ground cinnamon, if desired.

Makes 6 servings

COFFEE HOUSE INSPIRATIONS

fudge balls (page 196) are especially delicious when rolled in the following coatings: instant coffee, unsweetened cocoa, cookie crumbs, ground nuts, graham cracker crumbs, toasted coconut, *or* powdered sugar.

hot coffee float

Try this easy serving idea with different flavors of ice cream or frozen yogurt.

Prep: 5 minutes

¾ cup hot freshly brewed coffee

1 scoop coffee, chocolate, *or* vanilla ice cream

✦ **POUR** the coffee over the ice cream in a large cup or mug. Serve immediately.

Makes 1 serving

frozen "hot chocolate" coffee

This frozen version of hot chocolate coffee is sure to cool you down on a summer's night.

Prep: 10 minutes • Freeze: 4 ½ hours

3 cups half-and-half, divided

4 teaspoons instant coffee

½ cup granulated sugar

¼ cup light corn syrup

3 squares (3 ounces) unsweetened *or* semi-sweet chocolate

2 teaspoons vanilla extract

Whipped cream and chocolate curls (optional)

✦ **STIR** 2 cups of the half-and-half and the instant coffee in a medium bowl until well blended; set aside.

✦ **MICROWAVE** the remaining 1 cup of the half-and-half, sugar, corn syrup, and chocolate in a large microwavable bowl on High for 2 to 3 minutes stirring halfway through the cooking time. Stir until the chocolate is completely melted and the sugar is dissolved. Stir in the coffee mixture and the vanilla. Pour the mixture into a 9-inch square pan.

✦ **FREEZE** for about 1½ hours or until almost firm. Break up with a fork into small pieces. Freeze for about 3 hours longer or until firm. Break into small pieces. Spoon into chilled glasses. Top with whipped cream and chocolate curls, if desired. Serve with a spoon and a straw. Store the leftover dessert in the freezer.

Makes 4 servings

hot coffee float

midnight bliss
cake

For extra decadence, try a slice of this cake with a scoop of ice cream and a drizzle of Mexican Chocolate Sauce (page 195).

Prep: 10 minutes • Bake: 60 minutes

1 package (2-layer size) chocolate cake mix

1 package (4-serving size) chocolate flavor instant pudding and pie filling

2 tablespoons instant coffee

1 container (8 ounces) sour cream

4 large eggs

½ cup oil

½ cup cold brewed strong coffee

1 package (12 ounces) semi-sweet chocolate chips

Powdered sugar for sprinkling over the cake (optional)

✦ **HEAT** the oven to 350°F. Lightly butter and flour a 12-cup fluted tube pan or a 10-inch tube pan.

✦ **BEAT** all of the ingredients except the chocolate chips in a large bowl with an electric mixer set on low speed just until moistened, scraping the side of the bowl often. Beat on medium speed for 2 minutes or until well blended. Stir in the chocolate chips. Spoon the batter into the prepared pan.

✦ **BAKE** for 50 to 60 minutes or until a toothpick inserted near the center comes out clean. Cool in the pan for 10 minutes on a wire rack. Loosen the cake from the sides of the pan with a spatula or a knife. Gently invert the cake onto the rack. Cool completely. Sprinkle with powdered sugar, if desired. Cut into slices to serve.

Makes 12 servings

COFFEE HOUSE INSPIRATION

A light dusting of powdered sugar or cocoa powder can add a special look to the top of any dessert. Desserts and beverages topped with whipped cream or whipped topping look especialy nice sprinkled with cocoa powder. Place about 1 tablespoon of the powdered sugar or cocoa powder inside a small fine-meshed strainer. Hold the handle in one hand and gently tap the side of the strainer with the other hand to delicately sprinkle the powdered sugar or cocoa powder over the surface.

ice cream "tiramisu"

This frozen version of the classic dessert is very easy to make with coffee ice cream.

Prep: 10 minutes • Freeze: 3 hours

½ cup cooled freshly brewed double-strength
   coffee
2 tablespoons granulated sugar
2 tablespoons Marsala wine
1 teaspoon vanilla extract
24 hard ladyfingers
3 pints coffee ice cream (6 cups), softened
2 teaspoons unsweetened cocoa powder

✦ **MIX** the coffee, sugar, wine, and vanilla in a small bowl; set aside.

✦ **ARRANGE** half of the ladyfingers in the bottom of a 9-inch square dish. Brush the ladyfingers with half of the coffee mixture, allowing time for them to absorb the coffee mixture.

✦ **SPOON** half of the ice cream over the ladyfingers. Brush the remaining ladyfingers with the remaining coffee mixture. Place on top of the ice cream in the dish.

✦ **SPREAD** the remaining ice cream over the ladyfingers. Sift the cocoa powder over the ice cream.

✦ **FREEZE** for 3 hours or until firm. Let stand at room temperature for about 10 minutes or until the dessert can be cut easily. Cut into squares to serve. Store the leftover dessert in the freezer.

Makes 8 servings

COFFEE HOUSE INSPIRATION

For extra indulgence, serve squares of this dessert with the *mocha sauce* (page 45) or garnish with grated chocolate or chocolate curls (see our easy techniques on page 20).

candy bar shake

When you can't decide what to have—a candy bar or ice cream?

Prep: 5 minutes

¾ cup cold brewed strong coffee

4 triangles (⅓ of a 3.5 ounce bar) Swiss bittersweet *or* milk chocolate with honey and almond nougat, coarsely chopped

1 pint (2 cups) coffee, chocolate, *or* vanilla ice cream, slightly softened

✦ **PLACE** the coffee and chocolate in a blender container; cover. Blend on high speed until the chocolate is chopped into small pieces. Add the ice cream to the blender container; cover. Blend on high speed using on/off action until smooth. Pour into tall glasses. Serve immediately.

Makes 2 servings

cappuccino peanut butter snack mix

Here is a snack mix made to order for a night of television.

Prep: 5 minutes • Microwave: 1½ minutes

6 squares (6 ounces) semi-sweet chocolate

½ cup creamy peanut butter

6 cups spoon-sized shredded wheat cereal

3 envelopes instant cappuccino mix, any flavor

✦ **MICROWAVE** the chocolate and peanut butter in a large microwavable bowl on High for 1½ minutes, stirring halfway through the cooking time.

Stir until the chocolate is completely melted. Stir the cereal into the chocolate mixture until it is evenly coated.

✦ **PLACE** the cappuccino mixes in a large zipper-style plastic bag. Add the cereal mixture. Seal and shake the bag until the cereal is well coated. Store in a tightly covered container.

Makes about 7 cups

candy bar shake

mocha mania cookies

Serve these double chocolate cookies with a very tall glass of milk!

Prep: 5 minutes • Bake: 12 minutes

16 squares (16 ounces) semi-sweet chocolate,
  divided
¾ cup firmly packed brown sugar
¼ cup (½ stick) butter *or* margarine, softened
2 large eggs
2 tablespoons instant coffee
1 teaspoon vanilla extract
½ cup all-purpose flour
¼ teaspoon baking powder

◆ **HEAT** the oven to 350°F. Coarsely chop 8 squares
of the chocolate; set aside.

◆ **MICROWAVE** the remaining 8 squares of the
chocolate in a large microwavable bowl on High
for ½ minute or until the chocolate is almost
melted. Stir until the chocolate is completely
melted.

◆ **STIR** in the sugar, butter, eggs, instant coffee, and
vanilla. Beat with an electric mixer set on high
speed 30 seconds. Stir in the flour and baking powder. Stir in the reserved chopped chocolate. Drop
by scant ¼ cupfuls onto ungreased baking sheets.

◆ **BAKE** for 12 to 13 minutes or until the cookies are
puffed and feel set to the touch. Set the baking
sheet on wire racks to cool for 1 minute. Using a
metal spatula, transfer the cookies to the wire
racks. Cool completely. Store in a tightly covered
container.

Makes about 1½ dozen cookies

A DROP OF HISTORY

1921 The Cheek-Neal Coffee Company builds a new plant in Brooklyn, New York;
within 28 months Maxwell House coffee becomes the largest-selling coffee in
metropolitan New York.

java mini cakes

These little cupcakes are just the right size for a before bed snack.

Prep: 10 minutes • Bake: 25 minutes

1 package (2-layer size) chocolate cake mix
Cold brewed double-strength coffee
Java Pudding Frosting (below)

+ **HEAT** the oven to the temperature specified on the cake mix package. Place paper cupcake liners in 24 muffin cups.

+ **PREPARE** the cake mix as directed on the package, substituting the brewed coffee for the water. Spoon the batter into the paper-lined muffin cups, filling each cup about half full.

+ **BAKE** as directed on the package for cupcakes. Cool completely on a wire rack. Frost the cupcakes with Java Pudding Frosting. Store the frosted cupcakes in the refrigerator.

Makes 24 cupcakes

COFFEE HOUSE TIP

In this recipe, brewed coffee is substituted for the water in a cake mix. We've made cupcakes, but you can use the same technique to make a coffee-flavored 2-layer cake or a 13x9-inch cake.

java pudding frosting

Prep: 5 minutes

½ cup cold brewed double-strength coffee
½ cup cold milk
1 package (4-serving size) vanilla flavor instant pudding and pie filling
1 tub (8 ounces) frozen whipped topping, thawed

+ **POUR** the cold coffee and milk into a medium bowl. Add the pudding mix. Beat with a wire whisk for 1 minute. Gently stir in the whipped topping.

Makes about 4 cups frosting, *or* enough to frost 24 cupcakes, *or* one 13x9-inch cake, *or* fill and frost two 9-inch cake layers.

black & white
chocolate coffee

Semi-sweet and white chocolates are melted for this creamy, soothing beverage.

Prep: 5 minutes • Microwave: 1 ½ minutes

1 square (1 ounce) semi-sweet chocolate,
    chopped
1 square (1 ounce) white chocolate, chopped
1 cup half-and-half *or* whole milk
2 cups hot freshly brewed coffee
Whipped cream, ground cinnamon, and
    chocolate curls (optional)

✦ **MICROWAVE** the chocolates and half-and-half in a medium microwavable bowl on High for 1 to 1½ minutes, stirring after 1 minute. Whisk or stir until the chocolates are completely melted and the mixture is smooth. Stir in the coffee. Pour into large cups or mugs. Top each serving with whipped cream, cinnamon and chocolate curls, if desired.

Makes 6 servings

double capped
cappuccino

For a tasty mocha cappuccino, substitute hot chocolate milk for the hot milk.

Prep: 10 minutes

1 envelope instant cappuccino mix, any flavor
1 cup hot milk
Easy Cappuccino Topping (see Coffee House
    Inspiration on page 189)

✦ **PREPARE** the envelope of cappuccino mix as directed on the package, substituting the 1 cup hot milk for the water. Top with the Easy Cappuccino Topping. Serve immediately.

Makes 1 serving

black and white chocolate coffee

index